my **revisi⏻n** notes

AQA (A) AS
PSYCHOLOGY

Jean-Marc Lawton

(₂ HODDER
EDUCATION

With thanks to all the students whose valuable feedback helped develop this book.

Blackburn College	
BB36092	
BBfS	24.01.2014
150	£10.99

Hodder Education, an Hachette UK company, 338 Euston Road, London NW1 3BH

Orders

Bookpoint Ltd, 130 Milton Park, Abingdon, Oxfordshire OX14 4SB
tel: 01235 827827
fax: 01235 400401
e-mail: education@bookpoint.co.uk
Lines are open 9.00 a.m.–5.00 p.m., Monday to Saturday, with a 24-hour message answering service. You can also order through the Hodder Education website: www.hoddereducation.co.uk

© Jean-Marc Lawton 2012
ISBN 978-1-4441-5253-1

First printed 2012
Impression number 5 4 3 2
Year 2017 2016 2015 2014 2013 2012

Cover photo reproduced by permission of chrisharvey/Fotolia

Typeset by Datapage, India

Printed in India

Hachette UK's policy is to use papers that are natural, renewable and recyclable products and made from wood grown in sustainable forests. The logging and manufacturing processes are expected to conform to the environmental regulations of the country of origin.

P01970

Get the most from this book

Everyone has to decide his or her own revision strategy, but it is essential to review your work, learn it and test your understanding. These Revision Notes will help you to do that in a planned way, topic by topic. Use this book as the cornerstone of your revision and don't hesitate to write in it — personalise your notes and check your progress by ticking off each section as you revise.

☑ Tick to track your progress

Use the revision planner on pages 4 and 5 to plan your revision, topic by topic. Tick each box when you have:

● revised and understood a topic

● tested yourself

● practised the exam questions and gone online to check your answers and complete the quick quizzes

You can also keep track of your revision by ticking off each topic heading in the book. You may find it helpful to add your own notes as you work through each topic.

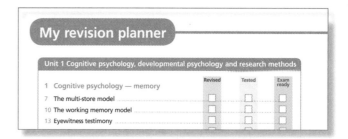

Features to help you succeed

Examiner's tips and summaries

Throughout the book there are tips from the examiner to help you boost your final grade.

Summaries provide advice on how to approach each topic in the exams, and suggest other things you might want to mention to gain those valuable extra marks.

Definitions and key words

Clear, concise definitions of essential key terms are provided on the page where they appear.

Key words from the specification are highlighted in bold for you throughout the book.

Typical mistakes

The examiner identifies the typical mistakes candidates make and explains how you can avoid them.

Now test yourself

These short, knowledge-based questions provide the first step in testing your learning. Answers are at the back of the book.

Exam practice

Practice exam questions are provided for each topic. Use them to consolidate your revision and practise your exam skills.

Online

Go online to check and print out your answers to the exam questions and try out the extra quick quizzes at **www.therevisionbutton.co.uk/myrevisionnotes**

My revision planner

Unit 1 Cognitive psychology, developmental psychology and research methods

Exam practice answers and quick quizzes at **www.therevisionbutton.co.uk/myrevisionnotes**

Unit 2 Biological psychology, social psychology and individual differences

Exam practice answers and quick quizzes at **www.therevisionbutton.co.uk/myrevisionnotes**

Countdown to my exams

6–8 weeks to go

- Start by looking at the specification — make sure you know exactly what material you need to revise and the style of the examination. Use the revision planner on pages 4 and 5 to familiarise yourself with the topics.

- Organise your notes, making sure you have covered everything on the specification. The revision planner will help you to group your notes into topics.

- Work out a realistic revision plan that will allow you time for relaxation. Set aside days and times for all the subjects that you need to study, and stick to your timetable.

- Set yourself sensible targets. Break your revision down into focused sessions of around 40 minutes, divided by breaks. These Revision Notes organise the basic facts into short, memorable sections to make revising easier.

Revised ☐

4–6 weeks to go

- Read through the relevant sections of this book and refer to the examiner's tips, examiner's summaries, typical mistakes and key terms. Tick off the topics as you feel confident about them. Highlight those topics you find difficult and look at them again in detail.

- Test your understanding of each topic by working through the 'Now test yourself' questions in the book. Look up the answers at the back of the book.

- Make a note of any problem areas as you revise, and ask your teacher to go over these in class.

- Look at past papers. They are one of the best ways to revise and practise your exam skills. Write or prepare planned answers to the exam practice questions provided in this book. Check your answers online and try out the extra quick quizzes at **www.therevisionbutton.co.uk/myrevisionnotes**

- Try different revision methods. For example, you can make notes using mind maps, spider diagrams or flash cards.

- Track your progress using the revision planner and give yourself a reward when you have achieved your target.

Revised ☐

One week to go

- Try to fit in at least one more timed practice of an entire past paper and seek feedback from your teacher, comparing your work closely with the mark scheme.

- Check the revision planner to make sure you haven't missed out any topics. Brush up on any areas of difficulty by talking them over with a friend or getting help from your teacher.

- Attend any revision classes put on by your teacher. Remember, he or she is an expert at preparing people for examinations.

Revised ☐

The day before the examination

- Flick through these Revision Notes for useful reminders, for example the examiner's tips, examiner's summaries, typical mistakes and key terms.

- Check the time and place of your examination.

- Make sure you have everything you need — extra pens and pencils, tissues, a watch, bottled water, sweets.

- Allow some time to relax and have an early night to ensure you are fresh and alert for the examinations.

Revised ☐

My exams

AS Psychology Unit 1

Date: ....

Time: ....

Location: ....

AS Psychology Unit 2

Date: ....

Time: ....

Location: ....

1 Cognitive psychology — memory

The multi-store model

The multi-store model (MSM) (Atkinson and Shiffrin 1968) explains how information in memory moves between three permanent storage systems: sensory memory, short-term memory and long-term memory. Each memory stage differs in terms of:

1 **capacity** — how much information can be stored

2 **duration** — how long information can be stored

3 **encoding** — the form in which information is stored

Information received via sensory organs enters **sensory memory**; only a fraction is attended to and sent for further processing in short-term memory. Unattended to sensory information either remains unprocessed or is immediately forgotten. Information actively processed through rehearsal is transferred to long-term memory for more permanent **storage** to await **retrieval** cues.

> **sensory memory** — a short duration store holding unprocessed impressions of sensory information received
>
> **storage** — the retention of information in memory
>
> **retrieval** — the extraction of stored information

Sensory memory
Revised ☐

Sensory memory (SM) uses separate sensory stores for each sensory input, for instance the **iconic store** for visual information and the **echoic store** for auditory information.

Trace decay results in information being rapidly lost from sensory memory. Information which has been attended to passes to short-term memory for more lasting representation.

> **Crowder (2003)** found that sensory memory retains information for a few milliseconds within the iconic store and about two to three seconds within the echoic store, suggesting the existence of separate sensory stores for each sensory input.
>
> **Sperling (1960)** found that the iconic store has a short capacity of 0.5 seconds, but a large capacity of 12 units of information.

> **Examiner's tip**
>
> Evidence that short-term memory and long-term memory are separate memory stores can be taken from two main sources. First, from research studies showing differences between the two in terms of encoding, storage and retrieval and second, from case studies showing two sorts of amnesia (memory loss) affecting two different brain areas: retrograde amnesia, which affects long-term memory and anterograde amnesia, which only affects short-term memory.

Short-term memory
Revised ☐

A temporary storage of information received from sensory memory, **short-term memory** (STM) is an active memory system holding information in use. It differs from long-term memory in terms of **duration**, **capacity**, **encoding** and how information is forgotten.

> **short-term memory** — a temporary store holding small amounts of information for brief periods
>
> **encoding** — the means by which information is represented in memory

Encoding in short-term memory

Information arrives in sensory memory in its original form (e.g. sound, vision etc.) and is encoded (represented) in a form short-term memory can deal with. The dominant form of encoding in STM is **acoustic** but other sensory codes are also used (e.g. **visual**).

> **Baddeley (1966)** found that participants given acoustically similar word lists e.g. 'cat' 'mat' etc. only recalled 15% of the words, indicating that there was acoustic confusion in short-term memory, which suggests that short-term memory is encoded on an acoustic basis.
>
> **Posner & Keele (1967)** found participants could work out that 'A' followed by 'A' were the same letters more quickly than if 'A' was followed by 'a'. As the visual code is different when 'A' is followed by 'a', it suggests that visual coding also occurs in short-term memory.

Capacity of short-term memory

The **capacity** of short-term memory is limited; research suggests a capacity of five to nine items. This is increased through chunking (see page 18).

> **Jacobs (1887)** gave participants either increasingly long lists of letters or numbers to recall, finding capacity for letters was 7 items and 9 items for numbers.
>
> **Miller (1956)** reviewed research studies, finding STM capacity to be between 5-9 items, but that the 'chunk' was the basic unit of STM, where information is grouped into meaningful units.

Duration of short-term memory

Duration is limited, being less than 30 seconds; research suggests that this information is rapidly lost if not rehearsed. Repetition retains material within the short-term memory loop, until eventually it becomes permanent within long-term memory.

> **capacity** — the amount of information that can be stored at a given time
>
> **duration** — the length of time information remains within storage

> **Peterson & Peterson (1959)** read participants nonsense trigrams (e.g. XQJ) and got them to count backwards in 3s for periods of between 3–18 seconds to prevent recall. Ninety percent of trigrams were recalled with a 3-second period, but only 5% with an 18-second period, implying short-term memory duration to be limited to about 20–30 seconds.
>
> **Marsh et al. (1997)** found short-term memory duration was brief if recall was unexpected, suggesting duration is dependent upon the degree of processing of information.

Long-term memory

Revised

Long-term memory (LTM) involves storing information over long periods, potentially a lifetime. Forgetting takes place due to problems retrieving memory traces rather than loss of information. Storage of information for longer than 30 seconds counts as LTM.

> **long-term memory** — a permanent store holding limitless amounts of information for long periods

Encoding in long-term memory

With verbal material, coding is mainly semantic (based on meaning); research indicates that encoding occurs in other forms too (e.g. visual and acoustic codes).

> **Baddeley (1966)** found participants given semantically similar word lists (words of similar meaning) could only recall 55% of the words after a 20-minute gap between presentation and recall, indicating there was semantic confusion in long-term memory, which suggests that it is encoded on a semantic basis.
>
> **Nelson & Rothbart (1972)** found participants made recall errors with homophones, words that sound the same, but have different meanings e.g. 'night' and 'knight', which suggests that acoustic encoding also occurs in long-term memory.

Typical mistake

In examinations students often make the mistake of using the wrong material to answer questions. This can be avoided by ensuring that you know what the 'command' words in questions mean and then presenting material that specifically suits such command words. For instance, 'outline' means to describe briefly (explanations or research studies), while 'evaluate' means to assess the effectiveness of such explanations and studies.

Exam practice answers and quick quizzes at **www.therevisionbutton.co.uk/myrevisionnotes**

Capacity of long-term memory

The potential capacity of long-term memory is unlimited. Although information can be lost due to decay and interference, such losses do not occur because of capacity limitation.

Anokhin (1973) estimated the number of possible neuronal connections in the human brain is 1 followed by 10.5 million kilometres of noughts and concluded that humans do not use all their brain potential, suggesting capacity of long-term memory is limitless.

Wagenaar (1986) tested himself on recall of 2,400 events listed in a diary over 6 years finding that recall was excellent, implying the capacity of long-term memory to be extremely large.

Duration of long-term memory

Memories can be lifelong and therefore their duration depends on lifespan. However, content has a longer duration if well-learned and some types of information also have a longer duration (e.g. information based on skills rather than facts).

Unlike short-term memory, information in long-term memory does not have to be continually rehearsed to be retained.

Bahrick et al. (1975) asked participants aged between 17–74 to identify ex-school friends from photos and name lists, finding those who left school within the last 15 years recalled 90% of faces and names, while those who'd left up to 48 years ago recalled 80% of names and 70% of faces, suggesting memory for faces is enduring.

Shephard (1967) found participants could recall pictures seen one hour ago when viewed among other pictures and still recalled 50% of them 4 months later, implying long-term memory to be long lasting.

Evaluation of the multi-store model
Revised

- The MSM was influential, inspiring research and led to later theories, like the working memory model, which offered greater understanding of how memory works. Research supports the existence of the separate memory stores of sensory memory, short-term memory and long-term memory.

- Shallice and Warrington (1970) reported on KF, who suffered brain damage that affected his short-term memory but not his long-term memory, while Scoville (1957) reported on an epileptic, HM, who had brain surgery that affected his long-term memory but not his short-term memory. This supports the idea of STM and LTM being separate stores.

- The model's idea of single STM and LTM stores is over-simplistic. Research indicates the existence of several STM stores, such as one for verbal and one for non-verbal sounds, and different types of LTM, like procedural, episodic and semantic memory stores.

- It focuses too much on describing the structure of memory (the three memory stores and the roles of attention and verbal rehearsal), neglecting the importance of memory processes.

- Cohen (1990) reported that memory capacity is best understood by reference to the *nature*, rather the *amount*, of information. Some items are easier to recall regardless of their quantity, but the model does not acknowledge this.

The working memory model

Essentially a theory of short-term memory, the working memory model (WMM) (Baddeley and Hitch 1974) questions the existence of a single STM store, perceiving STM as more complex than a temporary store for transferring information to long-term memory. STM is regarded as an 'active' store, holding several pieces of information while they are worked upon, hence 'working memory'.

Baddeley and Hitch proposed a multi-component WMM composed of: (1) a **central executive**, (2) a **phonological loop**, and (3) a **visual-spatial sketchpad**, based on the form of processing each carried out. A fourth component, the **episodic buffer** was added by Baddeley and Lewis in 1982.

Cohen (1990) described working memory as the focus of consciousness, holding information consciously thought about now.

The central executive   Revised ☐

The **central executive** (CE) acts as a filter, determining which information is attended to. The CE processes information in all sensory forms, directs information to other 'slave' systems and collects responses. It has limited capacity and deals with only one piece of information at a time.

> **central executive** — oversees and co-ordinates components of working memory

The CE selectively attends to particular types of information, attaining a balance between tasks when attention needs to be divided between them, for example talking while driving. The CE permits switching of attention between different information inputs.

> **D'Esposito et al. (1995)** used fMRI scans to find that the pre-frontal cortex was activated when verbal and spatial tasks were performed simultaneously, but not separately, implying that the brain area is linked to the central executive.
>
> **Baddeley (1996)** reported that participants could not generate random numbers whilst simultaneously alternating attention between letters and numbers, suggesting the two tasks were competing for central executive resources. This implies that the CE has limited capacity and can only handle one type of information at a time.

> **Examiner's tip**
>
> Research studies can be used to address both the 'outline' and 'evaluate' parts of essay-type l2-mark questions. Describing the aims, procedure, findings etc. is credited as *outlining*, while telling the examiner what the results mean using phrases like 'this suggests that...' or 'this supports the theory...' is credited as *evaluating*. Critical analysis of methodology can also count as evaluation.

The phonological loop   Revised ☐

The **phonological loop** (PL) and the visual-spatial sketchpad (see below) are 'slave' systems, temporary stores dealing with different kinds of sensory information.

> **phonological loop** — store of auditory information
>
> **phonological store** — part of the phonological loop that stores words we hear
>
> **articulatory process** — allows sub-vocal repetition of information in the phonological loop

The PL deals with auditory information and the order of information. It is like the rehearsal system of the multi-store memory, with a limited capacity determined by how much information is spoken aloud in around 2 seconds. As the PL is mainly an acoustic store, confusions can occur with similar sounding words.

Baddeley (1986) divided the PL into two sub-parts: (1) the **phonological store** (PS) and (2) the **articulatory process** (AP). The PS, or inner ear, stores words heard, while the AP, or inner voice, permits sub-vocal repetition of information retained in the PL.

> **Trojani & Grossi (1995)** reported on SC, who had brain damage that affected his phonological loop but not his visual-spatial sketchpad, implying the PL to be a separate system.
>
> **Baddeley et al. (1975)** found participants recalled more shorter words in serial order than longer words (the word length effect), suggesting that the capacity of the phonological loop is determined by how long it takes to say words, rather than the number of words.

The **primary acoustic store** (PAS) was added by Baddeley and Lewis (1981) after finding that memory of nonsense words is not affected by articulatory suppression, where learned words are prevented from being spoken aloud. Memory for nonsense words is thus dependent upon the PAS, which holds recently heard speech or sound.

> **primary acoustic store** — part of the phonological loop that stores recently heard speech or sound

> **Levy (1971)** reported that if participants were given concurrent auditory and visual material, articulatory suppression did not affect recall, suggesting that the primary acoustic store does exist.
>
> **Baddeley & Lewis (1982)** found that participants could identify which nonsense words were homophones (words that sound the same, but have different meanings like 'pane' and 'pain') while using their phonological loop for a different task, suggesting that the primary acoustic store is separate from the PL.

Visual-spatial sketchpad

Revised ☐

The **visual-spatial sketchpad** (VSS), or **inner eye**, handles non-phonological information and is a temporary store for visual and spatial items and the relationships between them; essentially it is a store for identified items and their location.

The VSS enables people to navigate, and interact with, their physical environment, with information being rehearsed and encoded through the use of 'mental pictures'.

> **visual-spatial sketchpad** — stores visual and spatial items
>
> **visual cache** — part of the visual-spatial sketchpad that stores visual material about form and colour
>
> **inner scribe** — part of the visual-spatial sketchpad that stores information about spatial relations

Logie (1995) suggests sub-dividing the VSS store further into (1) a **visual cache**, storing visual material about form and colour, and (2) an **inner scribe**, handling spatial relationships and rehearsing and transferring information in the visual cache to the central executive.

> **Gathercole & Baddeley (1993)** found participants could not simultaneously follow a moving point of light and describe the angles on a hollow letter 'F', as *both* tasks involved using the visual-spatial sketchpad. Other participants could follow the light and perform a simultaneous *verbal* task, as they involved using the VSS and the phonological loop, suggesting the VSS to be a separate slave system.
>
> **Klauer & Zhao (2004)** suggest that there is more interference between two visual tasks than between a visual and a spatial task, suggesting the existence of a separate visual cache and inner scribe.

The episodic buffer

Baddeley (2000) added a third 'slave' system, the **episodic buffer** (EB), because the model requires a general store to function efficiently. The central executive has no storage capacity and so cannot contain items relating to visual and acoustic properties. Thus the EB is a limited capacity store.

> **episodic buffer** — a limited capacity store of integrated information from the central executive, phonological loop, visual-spatial sketchpad and long-term memory

Prabhakaran et al. (2000) used fMRI scans to find greater right frontal brain activation for integrated verbal and spatial information, but greater posterior activation for unintegrated information, suggesting the existence of an episodic buffer that allows temporary retention of integrated information.

Alkhalifa (2009) found that problem-solvers using sequentially presented numbers (e.g. 1,2,3,4) were superior to those using parallel-presented material, where numbers on different parts of a screen had to be compared simultaneously. This suggests that the total capacity of working memory is larger than that determined by the capacity of the phonological loop and the visual-spatial sketchpad, implying the existence of the episodic buffer.

Evaluation of the working memory model

- Unlike the multi-store memory, the working memory model does not over-emphasise the importance of rehearsal for short-term memory retention.
- PET scans indicate that different brain areas are activated during verbal and visual tasks, supporting the idea of a working memory involving separate components.
- It is more plausible than the multi-store model as it demonstrates short-term memory in terms of temporary storage and active processing.
- Little is known about the central executive and this vagueness is used to explain all experimental results in a non-scientific, circular manner. For instance if two tasks are not performable simultaneously then the two processing components are seen as conflicting, or that the tasks exceed the CE's capacity. If two tasks can be performed simultaneously it is argued they do not exceed the available resources.
- Working memory concerns itself only with STM and so is not a comprehensive model of memory.
- Many of the findings supporting the WMM come from laboratory studies and may lack mundane realism.

> **Typical mistake**
>
> With the working memory model, possibly due to the sheer amount of descriptive material available, students often spend too much time outlining the theory at the expense of evaluating it. Remember that overall 50% of the marks are for analysis and evaluation, so ensure you spend as long learning/revising evaluations as you do descriptions. Plan your answers so that you know how much time to devote to each element.

Now test yourself

1 Explain what is meant by (i) encoding (ii) capacity (iii) duration?
2 Outline what is meant by STM and LTM, highlighting the differences between them.
3 What is the difference between the echoic and iconic stores in SM?
4 Make a list of evaluative points, both positive and negative, relating to the MSM.
5 Explain two positive and two negative criticisms of the WMM.

Answers on p. 102

Eyewitness testimony

Accuracy of eyewitness testimony

Revised

Convictions in law courts are often dependent on the accuracy of eyewitnesses' memories and yet in 75% of cases proven by DNA evidence to have been false convictions, guilty verdicts were based on inaccurate **eyewitness testimony** (EWT).

EWT research furthers understanding of how memory works and suggests how court cases should be conducted and testimonies gathered to facilitate accurate recall of events.

Bartlett (1932) showed that memories are not accurate 'snapshots' of events but are reconstructions influenced by active schemas (ready made expectations based on previous experiences, moods, existing knowledge, contexts, attitudes and stereotypes). Schemas are used to interpret the world, by filling in the gaps in knowledge of events and simplifying the processing of information.

Schemas have implications for the reliability of EWT, because witnesses do not merely recall facts as they occurred. Instead memories are reconstructed and biased by schemas active at the time of recall, including **post-event information**.

EWT is affected by experiences occurring after events are witnessed, a key factor being the use of **(mis)leading information**, particularly **(mis)leading questions** (see research boxes).

> **eyewitness testimony —** evidence provided by witnesses to a crime
>
> **post-event information —** misleading information added to questions after incidents have occurred
>
> **(mis)leading information / questions —** information / questions increasing the likelihood that participants' schemas influence them to give desired answers

Loftus & Palmer (1974) found participants asked to estimate the speed of cars in a film concerning traffic accidents were affected by being asked how fast the cars were going when they either contacted, hit, bumped, collided or smashed into each other, implying that leading questions affected participants' schemas, influencing them to give desired answers. More participants also remembered a week later seeing non-existent broken glass if given the verb 'smashed' rather than 'hit', suggesting that at recall misleading information is reconstructed with material from original memory.

Loftus (1975) found that 17% of participants watching a film of a car ride and asked 'how fast was the car going when it passed the white barn' (when there was no barn) one week later recalled seeing the barn. This shows the influence of post-event information, where misleading information is added to the question after incidents have occurred.

Evaluation of eyewitness testimony

Revised

- It is unclear with leading questions whether inaccuracies in recall are due to demand characteristics or genuine changes in memories of events. The consequences of inaccurate memories are minimal in research settings compared to real-life incidents. Foster et al. (1994) showed that eyewitness testimony was more accurate in real-life crimes than it was in simulations.

- Participants in research do not expect to be deliberately misled by researchers and therefore inaccurate recall should be expected.

- Misleading information affects only unimportant aspects of memory. Memory for important events is not easily distorted when information is obviously misleading.

Factors affecting the accuracy of recall

Anxiety

Revised ☐

Witnessing crimes can create anxiety and divert attention away from important features of a situation. The Yerkes-Dodson inverted-U hypothesis is used to explain this phenomenon: moderate amounts of **anxiety** improve the detail and accuracy of memory recall up to an optimal point, after which further increases in anxiety lead to a decline in recall.

The alternative Freudian explanation of **repression** suggests that anxiety impairs recall of memories. The act of forgetting is perceived to be motivated by the traumatic content of memories; access to such memories is denied in order to protect individuals from emotional distress.

> **anxiety** — an unpleasant state of emotional arousal

> **Examiner's tip**
>
> For candidates who wish to achieve high grades it is advisable to obtain material from multiple sources (e.g. textbooks and websites). Good quality answers offer a breadth of detailed information and elaborated evaluations, with points built up upon each other (e.g. using research studies that support or contradict each other).

Loftus et al. (1987) found that if a person is carrying a weapon, then a witness focuses on the weapon rather than the person's face, negatively affecting their ability to recall facial details of armed criminals and thus supporting the idea that anxiety can divert attention from important features of a situation.

Deffenbacher (1983) performed a meta-analysis of 21 studies examining the role of anxiety in the accuracy of eyewitness testimony, finding that heightened anxiety tended to negatively affect the memory of eyewitnesses. This suggests that anxiety can divert attention from important features of a situation.

Ginet & Verkampt (2007) found support for the Yerkes-Dodson inverted-U hypothesis, through producing moderate anxiety in participants by telling them fake electrodes gave electric shocks. Recall of minor details of a traffic accident viewed on film was superior to participants with low arousal, produced by being told the fake electrodes were purely for recording purposes. This implies that moderate anxiety does facilitate eyewitness testimony.

Koehler et al. (2002) found that participants were less able to recall stressful words than non-stressful words, lending support to Freud's concept of repression. However, Hadley & MacKay (2006) found stressful words were better recalled, as they were more memorable, suggesting that repression occurs sometimes, but not always.

Evaluation of anxiety

- Much research into anxiety and eyewitness testimony is laboratory based; in real life situations conflicting results occur. Yuille and Cutshall (1986) found witnesses to a fatal shooting with high arousal recalled fewer items correctly than those with lower levels, but witnesses with very high arousal had extremely accurate recall, suggesting support for the inverted-U hypothesis. However, Fruzetti et al. (1992) believes those with very high arousal had been closer to events, which assisted their recall.

- Deffenbacher (2004), reviewing his earlier findings, found them over-simplistic. He performed a meta-analysis of 63 studies, finding that eyewitness testimony performance increases gradually up to extremely high levels of anxiety, after which there is a catastrophic drop in performance incurring a negative impact on both accuracy of eyewitness identification and accuracy of recall of crime-related details.

Age

Revised

Cognitive abilities can diminish over time, suggesting that the accuracy of eyewitness testimony decreases with age. However, factors exist that moderate the effect of age upon the accuracy of recall: for instance children will accept inaccurate information from adults for fear of contradicting such authority figures, but have more accurate and detailed memories of events identified as serious.

There are issues relating to the accuracy of children's answers according to how they are questioned. Younger children are especially vulnerable to being misled by post-event information and leading questions.

Older people have less accurate and less detailed recall than young or middle-aged people and are more susceptible to misleading information. However, research findings from all age groups are not always consistent, possibly due to methodological flaws.

Krackow & Lynn (2003) found children aged between 4 and 6 years, who had been touched or not touched on various parts of their bodies, answered truthfully when asked directly, but wrongly 50% of the time when asked indirectly with a leading question, emphasising the vulnerability of young children to being misled by leading questions.

Poole & Lindsay (2001) found children aged 3 to 8 years included a lot of post-event information into recollections of a science demonstration, suggesting young children are especially affected by post-event information and thus provide more inaccuracies in eye witness testimonies.

Loftus et al. (1991) found elderly people were more likely to make false identifications, were poorer at recalling specific details and that elderly men in particular were prone to distortions through misleading post-event information, again suggesting that accuracy of recall declines with age and that the elderly are susceptible to misleading information.

Evaluation of age

- Usually older adults are compared with college students, on stimuli suited to college students. Anastasi and Rhodes (2006), testing recall of photographs previously seen, found that all participants performed best with photographs of their own age group, suggesting that stimuli used in research can influence findings.

- Elias et al. (1990) believes it is unclear why age effects occur. Younger adults may perform better as they are used to tests and more motivated to achieve. Some elderly people have associated poor physical health which impacts on memory.

- There are difficulties in controlling confounding variables when comparing different age groups (e.g. amount and type of education received). Also many studies use elderly people from nursing homes, who may be non-typical in having poor memory abilities and thus not form representative samples.

The cognitive interview

Components of the cognitive interview

Revised

Developed by Fisher and Geiselman (1992) the **cognitive interview** (CI) is a method of increasing the accuracy of eyewitness testimony recall in police interviews.

> **cognitive interview** — police interview procedure of witnesses that facilitates accurate, detailed recall

The CI is based on Tulving's (1974) idea that there are several retrieval paths to each memory and information not available through one technique may be accessible through another. Another principle behind the CI involves Tulving and Thomson's **encoding specificity theory** (1973), which suggests that memory traces consist of several features and using as many retrieval cues as possible enhances recall (see Table 1.1).

Table 1.1 Components of the Cognitive Interview

Change of narrative order	Recount the scene in different chronological orders, e.g. from end to beginning.
Change of perspective	Recount the scene from different perspectives, e.g. from the offender's point of view.
Mental reinstatement of context	Return to both the environmental and emotional context of the crime scene, e.g. weather and feelings.
Report everything	Recall all information, even if it appears to have little relevance or is accorded a lower level of confidence.

Context provides cues that increase feature overlap between initial witnessing and subsequent retrieval contexts, with context reinstatement involving emotional elements which work via state-dependent effects (e.g. returning to the scene of the crime and picturing how it smelt, what could be heard etc.) and sequencing elements, involving what was being done at the time.

The final element of the CI is reporting everything, as trivial incidents trigger more important memories. It is believed that change of narrative order and perspective aid recall because they reduce witnesses' use of prior knowledge, expectations and schemas, increasing eyewitness testimony accuracy.

Fisher et al. (1987) suggested an amended version of the CI known as the **enhanced cognitive interview** (ECI). Extra features include:

- minimisation of distractions
- reduction of anxiety
- encouraging the witness to speak slowly
- asking open-ended questions

> **enhanced cognitive interview** — advanced method of interviewing witnesses that overcomes problems of inappropriate sequencing of questions

Geiselman et al. (1985) found the cognitive interview procedure compared favourably against a standard interview technique and a hypnosis interview, suggesting the technique is valid.

Fisher et al. (1989) assessed the performance of police officers in gathering facts when using the enhanced cognitive interview compared to a standard interview technique, finding the ECI to be superior.

Ginet & Py (2001) found a significant increase in the quantity of correct information remembered by witnesses without a comparable increase in the number of errors, suggesting the cognitive interview is effective.

Milne & Bull (2002) found the 'report everything' and 'context reinstatement' components of the cognitive interview to be the key techniques in gaining accurate, detailed recall.

Geiselman & Fisher (1997) found that the cognitive interview works best when used within a short time following a crime rather than a long time afterwards

Evaluation of the cognitive interview

Revised

- It is composed of several techniques, with different police forces using different versions of it making comparisons and assessment difficult.

Exam practice answers and quick quizzes at **www.therevisionbutton.co.uk/myrevisionnotes**

- It can be time consuming, often requiring more time than police officers have available.
- Memon et al. (1993) reported officers believe the *'change of perspective'* component misleads witnesses into speculating about events witnessed and it is therefore less frequently used.
- The CI is recommended for use from 8 years upwards. Geiselman (1999) found that younger children recalled facts less accurately than with other interview techniques.
- The enhanced cognitive interview has proven an even more effective technique but is prone to producing false positives (incorrect items are remembered).

Now test yourself

Tested ☐

6   What are schemas and how can they affect EWT?

7   What have research studies revealed about the effects of leading questions on EWT?

8   How does the inverted-U hypothesis explain how anxiety affects recall?

9   Explain how repression can affect memory.

10   What have psychologists learned about the effect of age on recall?

11   What is the purpose of the cognitive interview [CI]?

12   Outline the components of the CI.

Answers on p. 102

Strategies for memory improvement

Psychological research has helped create techniques designed to improve recall.

Retrieval cues

Revised ☐

Retrieval cues are prompts that trigger recall. There are two types.

1 External (context-dependent) cues

Memory is affected by the physical environment where material is learnt. Research indicates that context-dependent cues facilitate recall i.e. people remember things best in the environment they were originally experienced.

> **Abernethy (1940)** tested participants' recall using a mixture of familiar and unfamiliar instructors and teaching rooms. Participants tested by a familiar instructor in a familiar room performed best, suggesting that familiar external cues are useful in improving recall.
>
> **Godden & Baddeley (1975)** asked divers to learn and recall word lists either on dry land or underwater. Results showed that words learnt and recalled in the same context were remembered best.

2 Internal (state-dependent) cues

The internal physiological state of an individual affects memory. Research suggests that having a similar internal environment as when information was encoded facilitates recall.

Examiner's tip

Research on context-dependent cues can be used by students in a practical way when studying and revising. Have a regular study area at home and when sitting examinations do so in a familiar manner, for example wearing your usual clothes, using familiar items, like pens and rulers. Memory is affected by external cues that relate to material learnt, so re-creating those cues will assist recall.

Overton (1972) found that participants who learned material when either drunk or sober recalled the material best when in the same internal state (drunk or sober) as when the information was encoded, implying that state-dependent cues aid recall.

Darley et al. (1973) found that participants who hid money while high on marijuana were more likely to recall the hiding place when in a similar drugged state, supporting the idea of state-dependent cues being an aid to recall.

Evaluation

● Many studies supporting cue-dependent recall are laboratory based, unlike everyday memory. The ability to do something previously learned (procedural memory) like riding a bike, for instance, is not affected by retrieval cues.

● Research has examined the effect of mood on recall; Ucros (1989) found a small state-dependent mood effect. However, most studies have proven inconclusive.

● Research supports the idea of cue-dependent forgetting being the prime reason for forgetting in long-term memory, demonstrating the importance of retrieval cues in memory recall.

Chunking
Revised

Short-term memory capacity can be increased by **chunking**, combining separate pieces of information into larger 'chunks' to make them more understandable by finding a common feature to group them together. For example, 19141918 can be 'chunked' to become the start and end dates of the First World War. Reading involves chunking letters into words and words into sentences.

chunking — a method of increasing short-term memory capacity by combining small pieces of information into larger units with a common feature

Simon (1974) found the size of chunks affected recall, where participants had a smaller span for bigger chunks than smaller chunks.

Baddeley et al. (1975) reported on the word-length effect, where the length of words being chunked affected recall, with participants recalling more short than long words.

Evaluation of chunking

● It shows that memory capacity may usefully be thought of in terms of units of organised information rather than individual pieces of information.

Mnemonics
Revised

Mnemonics are memory aids that assist recall, most commonly by organising material in some way, for instance structuring material to be recalled. Mnemonics work by allowing the storage of such structured material in a way that provides links to existing memories. Retrieval of a familiar item is then linked to the recall of less familiar items.

mnemonics — techniques that enhance recall of memory

Focusing on visual images involves visual imagery mnemonics (e.g. imagining a familiar route through the rooms of a house, where objects to be recalled are placed in sequence in different rooms; these objects are imagined within their visual placings, with recall assisted by individuals visualising taking the familiar route).

Focusing on words involves verbal mnemonics, for example using an acronym whereby an article to be recalled is formed from the first letters of other words: Every Good Boy Deserves Fun: E, G, B, D and F being notes used in musical annotation.

Marston & Young (1974) compared visual and verbal mnemonic techniques in remembering word lists, finding that verbal strategies produced equal recall of items classed as of 'high imagery' and 'medium imagery', while visual strategies resulted in higher performance for 'high imagery' words, but lower performance for 'medium imagery' words. This suggests that the best choice of strategy depends upon the type of information being recalled.

Baltes & Kleigl (1992) found that older adults prefer verbal rather than visual mnemonics, as they increasingly find it harder to produce and recall visual images. This suggests that the ability to use different forms of mnemonics changes through life.

Bower & Clarke (1969) found that participants using narrative stories to help recall lists of nouns in the correct order remembered 93% of the material compared to only 13% for participants not using narrative stories, suggesting verbal mnemonics to be a powerful aid to memory.

Evaluation of mnemonics

- People differ in their abilities to visualise, and therefore the usefulness of visual imagery is dependent on whether a person is a 'high-imager' or a 'low-imager'.

- Visual imagery mnemonics are limited as they often only work when trying to learn and recall actual objects rather than abstract concepts and ideas.

Active processing

Revised

The term **active processing** refers to procedures in which a learner goes beyond mere passive, unthinking encoding of information and instead subjects material to deep and meaningful processing.

active processing — subjecting information to deep and meaningful analysis

Craik & Lockhart (1972) found that if participants analysed material semantically by its meaning, recall was improved, implying that semantic processing draws upon many varied associations within long-term memory. Recall becomes easier as more recall pathways are established.

Morris et al. (1985) found that football fans recalled more scores than non-fans, because they actively processed the information (e.g. comparing scores to expected ones and calculating the impact upon league positions). This suggests that active processing is an effective strategy for memory improvement.

Evaluation of active processing

- This is an untestable and non-scientific **circular** concept, as not only is strongly-processed information regarded as being recalled better but also well-recalled information is presumed to have been actively processed.

- Active processing is a dynamic theory, seeing memory as a process not a set of passive stores. It provides meaningful associations between memory and other cognitive areas.

Now test yourself

13 Give a concise, detailed outline for each of the following:
(i) retrieval cues (ii) chunking
(iii) mnemonics (iv) active processing.

Answers on p. 102

Tested

Exam practice

1 Select from the list below to complete the table relating to the MSM. [4]

capacity   acoustic   unlimited
repression   semantic   phonological loop

	STM	LTM
?	5 – 9 items	?
Duration	30 seconds	Up to a lifetime
Encoding	?	?

2 Outline one strength and one limitation of the MSM. [2 + 2]

3 Sionag finds that when her music teacher plays her a lengthy piece of unfamiliar music and asks her to play it back, she has difficulty recalling it all.

   (a) Explain using the MSM why this should be so. [3]

   (b) Devise a strategy Sionag could use to help her remember the piece of music. [3]

4 Describe the main features of the WMM. [6]

5 Explain one strength and one weakness of the WMM. [3 + 3]

6 Explain how misleading information can affect the accuracy of EWT. [4]

7 'Eyewitness testimony has time and time again been shown to be unreliable and should not be used to convict criminals'.

   Discuss what psychological research has revealed about the accuracy of EWT. [12]

8 One of the following is a leading question:

   (a) Did you see the red barn?

   (b) Did you see a red barn?

   Identify which of the above is a leading question and explain why it is a leading question. [1 + 2]

9 Steve is an experienced police officer with special responsibility for interviewing witnesses. He has recently been on a course to train him in how to use the cognitive interview technique, where he was encouraged to always make witnesses feel comfortable and at ease and to encourage witnesses to recall events in different ways, such as by recounting a scene from end to beginning or from the viewpoints of other witnesses. He was also told that witnesses should recall any feelings they had and the environmental conditions, such as the weather, and that all memories of an event, however minor or unclear they seem, should be recalled.

   (a) Refer to features of the scenario above to identify components of the cognitive interview. [6]

   (b) Explain one limitation of using the cognitive interview. [2]

10 (a) Outline two strategies for improvement of memory. [3 + 3]

   (b) Evaluate one of the strategies for memory improvement outlined in part (a). [5]

Answers and quick quiz 1 online

Online

Examiner's summary

✔ The multi-store model explains how information in memory moves between three permanent storage systems; better prepared students will be able to relate evidence showing how short-term and long-term memory differ in terms of encoding, storage and retrieval and that amnesia affects STM or LTM, but not both.

✔ The working memory model sees STM as comprising several active stores that act upon material as it is worked upon; students should be able to outline, as well as to evaluate, the roles of these individual stores.

✔ Eyewitness testimony suggests that memory is not necessarily accurate and can be affected by misleading information.

✔ Research has led to strategies that improve memory (e.g. retrieval cues, chunking and active processing) which can be used by students to improve studying and revising.

✔ Students should be aware of research which shows EWT to be influenced by anxiety and age factors in both descriptive and evaluative terms.

✔ Students should be aware of how the cognitive interview can increase the accuracy of EWT in police interviews.

2 Developmental psychology — early social development

Explanations of attachment

An **attachment** is usually formed between a parent and a child, developing in set stages within a fairly rigid timescale. Schaffer (1977) sees attachments developing in three stages: (1) newborn: predisposed to attach to any person, (2) baby: learns to distinguish primary and secondary caretakers but accepts care from anyone, (3) attachment behaviour is focused upon a single carer.

> **attachment** — a two-way enduring emotional tie to a specific other person

The manner in which carers interact with infants, especially in fearful situations, shapes the nature of attachments.

> **Examiner's tip**
>
> Candidates may be asked to outline/define what is meant by attachment. Make sure you can do this sufficiently to earn all the marks on offer. If a question is worth 3 marks you should be able to answer it correctly and elaborate the answer (provide detail) to achieve all the marks. Practise writing such answers as part of your revision.

There are two main explanations of attachment.

1 Learning theory   Revised ☐

Learning theory sees behaviour developing through experience via the process of association, with children developing attachments to those who feed them.

> **learning theory** — the belief that children develop attachments to feeders through a process of association

- **Classical conditioning** occurs where a **stimulus** becomes associated with a **response**. With attachments this involves babies learning to associate caregivers with food, an **unconditioned or primary reinforcer**, due to the pleasure food gives, with caregivers being a **conditioned** or **secondary reinforcer**. Because caregivers satisfy babies' physiological needs, learning theory is also known as **cupboard love theory**.

Caregivers become rewarding by themselves, with babies feeling secure in their presence without the need for food.

- **Operant conditioning** involves learning behaviour due to its consequences via the use of **reinforcements** (stimuli presented after responses that increase the likelihood of the responses recurring). With attachments, caregivers become associated with reducing unpleasant sensations of hunger and thus become a source of reinforcement (reward).

> **Examiner's tip**
>
> The specification lists two theories of attachment, the learning theory and the evolutionary perspective. You should therefore be able both to describe (outline) and evaluate these theories in depth as either or both could be asked about in the examination. Knowledge of additional theories, like the psychodynamic theory, could be used as evaluation in longer essay-type questions.

Dollard & Miller (1950) calculated that babies are fed 2,000 times by their main carer in their first year, more than sufficient for carers to act as a form of negative reinforcement by becoming associated with removing unpleasant sensations of hunger in line with learning theory.

Schaffer & Emerson (1964) interviewed mothers about their babies' behaviour in separation situations, like being left alone or put to bed, finding they often formed attachments to people not involved in their physical care, such as fathers. In 39% of cases the main carer, usually the mother, was not the main attachment figure, implying feeding not to be the primary explanation of attachment.

Fox (1977) reported on attachments between mothers, children and metapelets on Israeli kibbutz. Metapelets provide full-time care for newborns, allowing mothers to work, though some time is spent with parents. Children were more attached to their mothers, some having little or no attachment to the metapelets. As metapelets did most feeding, this suggests learning theory is flawed.

Evaluation of learning theory

- Schaffer (1971) argued that cupboard love theories put things the wrong way round. Babies do not 'live to eat' but 'eat to live', thus are active seekers of stimulation, not passive recipients of nutrition.

- Bowlby (1973) believed infants only occasionally require food but always require the protection of emotional security that closeness to attachment figures provides. This implies that food is not the main explanation for formation of attachments.

- Conditioning explains the development of simple behaviours but attachments are complex behaviours with intense emotional components. The fact that attachments also develop with non-feeders weakens support for the learning theory.

- Learning theory ignores the considerable evidence highlighting the role of evolutionary aspects of attachment, thus weakening the theory's importance.

Typical mistake

One common mistake is to confuse Freud's psychodynamic theory with the behaviourist learning theory, as both are cupboard love theories. This is because they both involve children forming attachments to those who feed them. However they adopt very different viewpoints as to why attachments to feeders form, so do not confuse them or see them as one theory.

2 Bowlby's theory — (1951) (1969) (1973)

Revised

Bowlby's theory rejected cupboard love theory, perceiving attachment instead as a human form of **imprinting**. This is an innate behaviour (requiring no learning) which some neonate animals show by following the first moving object encountered during a set time period (*critical period* see below).

Bowlby saw imprinting as keeping infants safe from danger by remaining close to caregivers, an attachment behaviour evolved through **natural selection** as it enhanced survival.

Attachment behaviours include **social releasers**, like crying and smiling, which maintain parental attention, as well as following behaviour to maintain physical closeness. Such behaviours function in an automatic, stereotyped manner, triggered initially by anyone. However, over time they become focused on fewer individuals and organised into more flexible, sophisticated behaviour systems.

Evolutionary theory sees attachment as a two-way complimentary process, whereby carers innately respond to infants' signals, with babies displaying **monotropy**, an innate tendency to attach to the adult who interacts with them most sensitively, usually the biological mother.

Bowlby's theory — attachments form from an innate ability to keep close proximity to caregivers

imprinting — a form of attachment where offspring follow the first large moving object encountered

monotropy — an innate tendency to become attached to one specific person

social releasers — infant social behaviours stimulating adult interaction and caregiving

Bowlby sees attachment as a **control system** orientated to maintain a 'steady state' of being close to the main carer (mother). When the steady state is threatened, such as by the mother's absence or the presence of strangers, attachment behaviours are activated to restore it. Bowlby perceived a **critical period** for the formation of attachments. He saw mothering as useless for most children if delayed until after 12 months and useless for all children if delayed until after 2.5–3 years.

The maternal attachment is the first and strongest bond to develop, forming an **internal working model** upon which later adult relationships, vital for reproduction, will be built.

> **Lorenz (1935)** imprinted newly hatched goslings onto himself, finding that certain animals have innate tendencies to respond to specific forms of stimuli (e.g. vocalisations) displayed by adults. Such innate 'pre-programming' incurs an evolutionary advantage through keeping youngsters safe by maintaining close proximity with their protectors.
>
> **Rutter (1981)** found mothers are not special in the way Bowlby perceived them to be. Babies exhibit many attachment behaviours towards various attachment figures other than mothers, with no specific attachment behaviour used explicitly towards mothers. This weakens support for the evolutionary perspective.
>
> **Lamb (1982)** found attachments to different people, like grandparents, siblings etc. fulfilled different purposes, for instance going to father for play but grandmother for comfort. Therefore attachments are not seen as a hierarchy with 'mother' at the top, going against the concept of monotropy.

Evaluation of Bowlby's theory

Imprinting applies mainly to **precocial** animals (those mobile soon after birth) therefore attachment may not simply be a human form of imprinting.

- Schaffer and Emerson (1964) believed attachments are most likely with individuals showing **sensitive responsiveness** (those who identify and respond appropriately to infants' needs). This goes against Bowlby's conceptualisation of attachment as human imprinting, whereby mere exposure to an adult is sufficient for attachment to occur.

- Evidence supports aspects of Bowlby's theory, like the continuity hypothesis, as consistency is found between early attachment experiences and later relationships.

Types of attachment

Initial research was conducted by Ainsworth in Uganda and later in Baltimore, USA using the **strange situation** testing procedure, an observational technique assessing the quality of mother–child pair relationships.

The strange situation examines how infants aged between 9 and 18 months behave during eight episodes of mild stress and novelty, especially during separation from mother, the presence of strangers and reunion scenarios.

Attachment behaviour was recorded in five categories: (i) proximity and contact seeking behaviours, (ii) contact maintaining behaviours, (iii) proximity and interaction avoiding behaviours, (iv) contact and interaction resisting behaviours, (v) search behaviours.

critical period — a time period within which attachments must form

Examiner's tip

To gain a better understanding of Bowlby's theory of monotropy it would be a good idea to have a working knowledge of evolutionary theory (Darwin), especially the role of natural selection, as Bowlby's theory has a strong evolutionary basis to it.

Typical mistake

Bowlby's theory of monotropy is an *explanation* of attachment, while his maternal deprivation hypothesis concerns the *effects* of disrupting attachments. However, students often confuse the two and while they do overlap, they should generally be used separately to answer specific questions about different aspects of attachment. Know which theory is which.

sensitive responsiveness — perceiving and responding appropriately to infants' needs

Typical mistake

Students often perform poorly not because their knowledge is poor but because they do not understand the terms used in exam questions. For instance, 'outline' means to describe (theories and studies), while 'evaluate' means to assess the value or effectiveness of such theories/ studies. Learn what these terms mean and require and always read questions fully before answering them.

strange situation — an observational testing procedure measuring the quality of attachments

Attachment styles

Revised

Three main attachment styles were identified:

1 Securely attached (Type B). Children are willing to explore, display high stranger anxiety, easy to soothe and enthusiastic at return of caregiver. Caregivers are sensitive to their charges.

2 Insecure–avoidant (Type A). Children are willing to explore, display low stranger anxiety, indifferent to separation and avoid contact at the return of caregiver. Caregivers often ignore their charges.

3 Insecure–resistant (Type C). Children are not willing to explore, display high stranger anxiety, show distress at separation and seek and reject contact at return of caregiver. Caregivers are ambivalent, displaying simultaneous opposite feelings and behaviours.

4 Ainsworth concluded there are two distinct features of attachment: firstly that infants seek proximity to mothers, especially when feeling threatened, and secondly that secure attachments permit infants to explore from a secure base, essential for cognitive and social development.

5 Sensitive responsiveness is essential in determining the quality of attachments and involves correctly identifying and responding to a child's needs. Sensitive caregivers tend to have securely attached babies, while insensitive mothers have insecurely attached babies.

> **Examiner's tip**
>
> The specification explicitly refers to the strange situation, which thus could feature directly in examination questions. Therefore candidates must have a working knowledge of the technique and be aware of its strengths and weaknesses in order to evaluate it. Although Ainsworth is not referred to explicitly in the specification, she is associated so closely with the strange situation that it is essential to be aware of her research.

Ainsworth et al. (1978) used the strange situation to assess attachment relationships in 106 mother–child pairs, with the category of behaviour displayed being recorded and scored on an intensity scale of 1 to 7 every 15 seconds. Interviews were also conducted with mothers. 70% of pairs were securely attached, 15% had insecure–avoidant attachment type and 15% had insecure–resistant attachment type.

Main and Solomon (1986) found an additional attachment type, insecure–disorganised (Type D), displayed by a small number of children whose behaviour is a confusing mixture of approach and avoidance behaviours.

Main et al. (1985) found 100% of infants securely attached before 18 months were still securely attached at 6 years, and 75% of those who had been anxious–avoidant remained so, suggesting the strange situation is reliable, as children tested at different times generally demonstrate identical attachment types.

Evaluation of strange situation

Revised

- It has become the **paradigm** (accepted method) of identifying and measuring attachment styles.

- Van Ijzendoorn and Schuengel (1999) reported that Ainsworth's belief that parental sensitivity determined attachment security was supported by later studies using larger samples, demonstrating the value of Ainsworth's research and its important contribution to psychological knowledge.

- It artificially assesses attachment, being laboratory-based with mothers and strangers acting to a 'script' unrelated to normal situations and therefore lacking in **ecological validity**. Brofenbrenner (1979) found

> **paradigm** — an accepted method
> **ecological validity** — findings that can be generalised to real-life settings

infants' attachment behaviours are much stronger in a laboratory than at home.

- The strange situation is accused of lacking validity as it may be measuring individual relationships rather than attachment types. Main and Weston (1981) found children can display different attachment types to different people (e.g. being insecurely attached to mother but securely attached to father) demonstrating that attachment patterns display qualities of distinct, individual relationships, rather than universal characteristics of all relationships.

- The strange situation assumes attachment types are fixed characteristics of children, but classification can change if family circumstances, like mothers' stress levels, alter. Therefore attachment style is not a permanent characteristic.

- Many mothers do leave children briefly with strangers, like babysitters and childminders, but it can nonetheless be regarded as unethical to use a research method that deliberately stresses children by exposure to strangers in order to study attachment patterns.

Cultural variations in attachment

If, as Bowlby believed, attachments evolved due to their survival value, then attachment patterns should be the same across cultures, regardless of differences in childrearing practices, with secure attachments predominant. If attachment patterns vary across cultures, it would suggest that attachments are environmentally determined through different childrearing practices.

However, if attachment patterns do vary cross-culturally this could still be explained via evolution. For instance Belsky (1999) argued that insecure attachment types are associated with weak adult relationships and early sexual activity, useful characteristics in environments with a high death rate, as reproduction would need to occur at a young age, without emotional attachments forming to people who may die young.

Childrearing styles do vary considerably cross-culturally; in some cultures one person does the majority of caregiving while in others many carers are involved. There are also cross-cultural variations in how attachment types are perceived. What in our culture is regarded negatively as an insecure–avoidant attachment type is seen as an independent attachment type in Germany, a culture where independence is positively valued. Not surprisingly a higher proportion of insecure–avoidant attachment type is found in Germany.

Cross-cultural studies show differences both *within* and *between* cultures. However, such studies tend to use the strange situation testing procedure, which may not be suitable for use in all cultures and can therefore produce misleading results.

McMahon et al. (2001) used the strange situation to compare 42 mother–child pairs from the Dogon people of Mali, where constant physical proximity, breastfeeding on demand and immediate response to distress are the norm, with 306 mother–child pairs from North America, finding a higher proportion of secure attachments among the Dogon sample and no insecure–avoidant attachment types. The results are explicable by the incompatability of Dogon childrearing practices with practices associated with avoidant styles in Western cultures, as in Dogon culture there's no maternal rejection of attachment bids, intrusion or lack of physical contact. The results suggest that naturally parented children have greater attachment security.

Tomlinson et al. (2005) studying a South African sample of naturally parented children and Zevalkink et al. (1999), using a similar Indonesian sample, also found high levels of secure attachment and low levels of avoidant attachment, lending support to McMahon's findings.

Van Ijzendoorn & Kroonenberg (1988) reviewed 32 strange situation studies from eight countries, involving over 2,000 children, finding a similar pattern to Ainsworth, with secure attachment the most common type, followed by insecure–avoidant and insecure–resistant. Insecure–avoidant was not common in Japan or Israel, but insecure–resistant was, with marked differences between the two Japanese studies reviewed. In one there were no insecure–avoidant children, while in the other, the pattern was like that found by Ainsworth, suggesting there are differences not only between cultures but within cultures.

Kyoung (2005) found differences between Americans and Koreans, with Korean infants not staying close to mothers and Korean mothers being more likely to play with infants when returning from a separation, but as there was a similar proportion of securely-attached children in both cultures, it suggests different childrearing practices can lead to secure attachments.

Evaluation of cultural variations Revised ☐

- The greater frequency of the insecure–resistant attachment type in Japan may result from stress during the strange situation due to infants' unfamiliarity at being left with strangers. Japanese children are rarely separated from mothers, so separation is upsetting for them. Contrastingly Rogoff (2003) found black American children have many caregivers and are encouraged to be friendly to strangers, thus the strange situation activated their interest to explore. This shows that the strange situation has different meanings in different cultures and childrearing practices need to be scrutinised in order to interpret findings based on the technique.

- Within collectivist cultures, sociability is not regarded as a type of social competence. Okonogi (1992) reported that Japanese children are taught to fear and avoid strangers, which suggests the strange situation is not an appropriate research method for non-western cultures, as it is based on Western cultural practices.

- Attachment patterns vary cross-culturally and the strange situation is not applicable in all cultures; this suggests that attachment theory is culture-bound, having reference only to Western cultures.

- The strange situation contains procedural elements unknown to some cultures (like the unfamiliarity of Dogon children being left with strangers) leading to a risk of such children being wrongly classified as insecurely attached.

- There is a danger with cross-cultural studies of attachment of an **imposed etic** (where investigators conduct research and interpret results in ways that are biased in terms of their own cultural beliefs). Wrongly imposing such views onto other cultures can lead to false results and conclusions.

Examiner's tip

An effective way of evaluating cultural variations in attachment is to focus on the methodology of cross-cultural studies, as there are many relevant factors (e.g. cultural bias and imposed etic). This is best achieved by giving specific examples of where such factors occur (e.g. McMahon's (2001) study of the Dogon people where inappropriate usage of the strange situation occurred).

Now test yourself

Tested ☐

1 What is an attachment?
2 How does learning theory explain the formation of attachments through (i) classical conditioning (ii) operant conditioning?
3 Does research support learning theory? Give details.
4 How does Bowlby explain the development of attachments?
5 Does research support Bowlby? Give details.
6 Describe the following attachment types: (a) secure (b) insecure–avoidant (c) insecure–resistant (d) insecure–disorganised.
7 What evaluative points can be made about the 'strange situation'?
8 Compile an evaluation of cultural variations in attachment.

Answers on p. 102

Disruption of attachment

The maternal deprivation hypothesis (Bowlby 1946, 1956)

Revised ☐

The **maternal deprivation hypothesis** (MDH) came out of Bowlby's theory of monotropy, whereby if attachment failed to develop to a maternal figure, or formed and subsequently broken, then serious, irreversible long-term damage to children's emotional and intellectual would occur (e.g. **affectionless psychopathy** where individuals do not develop social conscience due to maternal deprivation in the first two years of life).

The MDH was formed from research undertaken in the 1930s and 1940s of children raised in orphanages and residential nurseries, where Bowlby perceived deprivation of maternal care as the common factor leading to negative outcomes (e.g. poor IQ scores).

affectionless psychopathy — lacking a social conscience

maternal deprivation hypothesis — the belief that disruption to attachment incurs serious, irreversible negative effects

Goldfarb (1943) compared children raised in institutional care in social isolation, with children raised in foster homes, finding that the institutionalised children scored more poorly on measure of sociability, social maturity, abstract thinking and rule following. By age 14 the institutional children had an average IQ of 72 compared to the fostered children's 95, suggesting that institutional care damages social and intellectual development.

Bowlby (1944) studied 44 juvenile thieves, comparing them with non-thieves with emotional problems, finding 32% of the thieves were affectionless psychopaths possessing no social conscience, while 0% of the non-thieves exhibited this condition. Also 86% of the affectionless psychopaths had endured maternal separation, compared to only 17% of thieves who weren't affectionless psychopaths. The results imply maternal separation incurs long-term, serious consequences.

Spitz (1945,1946) reported on children raised in poor quality South American orphanages where untrained staff were overworked, rarely having time to speak to, play with or give affection to the children. The children displayed anaclitic depression, a reaction to the loss of a love object characterised by fear, sadness, crying, social withdrawal, loss of appetite, weight loss and developmental retardation, implying that disruption of attachments has grave negative consequences, both physically and psychologically.

Evaluation of the maternal deprivation hypothesis

- Goldfarb (1943) did not use random samples so the fostered children may have been naturally brighter, more sociable and healthier than the institutionally raised children, explaining why they were fostered rather than placed in care.

- Children's homes/orphanages tended to provide unstimulating environments, which may explain retarded development rather than the lack of maternal care.

- Bowlby (1944) confused privation with deprivation. Institutional care tended to be concerned with privation where no attachments ever formed, rather than deprivation where attachments had formed and were broken.

Deprivation
Revised

The term **deprivation** refers to the loss of an attachment or attachment figure and includes both short-term and long-term separations.

> **deprivation** — separation from attachment figures

Examples of short-term separations include:
- hospitilisation of infant or attachment figure
- attachment figure goes to work while infant has childminder/daycare
- holidays
- short-term imprisonment

Bowlby (1969) described the components of distress caused by short-term separation as:

1 **Protest** — a direct expression of a child's anger, fear, bitterness and confusion that is an immediate reaction to separation. Characterised by crying, struggling to escape or clinging to the mother to prevent her leaving.

2 **Despair** — a calmer, apathetic form of behaviour, with little reaction to offers of comfort. Anger and fear are experienced internally, while a child comforts itself (e.g by thumb-sucking).

3 **Detachment** — a wary form of behaviour, people being cautiously responded to. Caregivers may be rejected on their return and subjected to fits of anger.

Examples of long-term separations include:

- death of attachment figure
- divorce resulting in separation
- adoption
- institutionalisation (children's home etc.)
- long-term imprisonment

Robertson & Robertson (1971) made a series of films about children undergoing short-term separations in hospital, finding their distress tended to follow Bowlby's three components of protest, despair, detachment. Effects were noticeable for long periods after reunion with caregivers, such as tantrums, demonstrating the long-term nature of the damage.

Douglas (1975) found that for children aged 4, separations of less than a week were correlated with behavioural difficulties, supporting Bowlby's maternal deprivation hypothesis.

Quinton & Rutter (1969) found that adolescents who had endured short-term hospitalisation separations from attachment figures in the first 5 years of life had more behavioural problems than adolescents who had not been similarly separated, suggesting that such effects are real and long term.

Evaluation of short-term deprivation

- Robertson and Robertson (1971) showed that the negative effects of short-term separation were avoidable by providing children with an alternative attachment and their usual home routine, demonstrating that negative consequences are not inevitable.

- Radical changes to hospital routines occurred due to the Robertsons' research. Shift rotas were set so that children had regular contact with the same nurses, allowing provision for alternative attachments to form, visiting hours allowed regular contact with caregivers and children were encouraged to bring familiar objects/toys with them.

- Barrett (1997) believes individual differences in reactions to short-term separation are not considered. Securely attached children and more mature children cope well with separations, implying that it is only certain children that experience distress.

Schaffer (1996) found that most children were negatively affected by divorce, at least in the short term, demonstrating the wide-ranging effects of deprivation.

Hetherington & Stanley-Hagan (1999) found that 25% of children experienced long-term adjustment problems to divorce, though most eventually adapt, implying negative developmental outcomes are more short than long term.

Furstenberg & Kiernan (2001) found children of divorced parents scored lower than children of non-divorced parents on measures of social development, emotional well-being, self-concept, academic performance, educational attainment and physical health, suggesting that divorce has wide-ranging negative effects on children's development.

Evaluation of long-term deprivation

- It is logical that long-term rather than short-term deprivation incurs stronger negative consequences and research supports this view.

- Demo and Acock (1996) found wide reactions to divorce, with some children actually developing stronger attachments to parents after divorce, possibly due to the removal of the stressful environment of marital conflict and parents being more attentive and supporting to children after divorcing. This demonstrates that negative consequences are not inevitable.

● Research into long-term deprivation allowed psychologists to develop coping strategies, like those helping children to deal with divorce. Some American states even require divorcing parents to attend training programmes, tutoring them in strategies such as providing emotional warmth and keeping to consistent rules.

Privation

The term **privation** refers to attachment bonds never having formed. This differs from deprivation, where a bond does form but then is broken.

> **privation** — never having formed an attachment

Several case studies have investigated whether children enduring extreme privation can recover and if so, to what extent. Privation is likelier than deprivation to incur permanent emotional damage like affectionless psychopathy. Studies of institutional children are regarded as cases of privation as they do not usually have opportunities to form attachments.

The results of case studies can be contradictory, with some individuals demonstrating full recovery while others show little if any progress.

Tizard & Hodges (1978) performed a longitudinal study of children placed in institutional care with no opportunities to form attachments and too young to have formed attachments with their mothers. Some of the children remained in care, some were adopted and some returned home. There was also a control group of normally raised children. Those experiencing institutional care had problems with peer relationships, suggesting privation has harmful consequences. However, adopted children developed close attachments with adoptive parents, demonstrating that negative effects are not inevitable.

Koluchova (1972,1991) reported on twin boys cruelly treated by their stepmother. Discovered at age 7 they were physically underdeveloped, lacked speech and were scared of adults. At age 14, after being adopted by nurturing sisters, their social, emotional, physical and intellectual functioning was normal and this continued into adulthood, demonstrating that privation effects are not necessarily permanent.

Freud & Dann (1951) reported on orphans who survived Nazi concentration camps, brought to Britain with little language ability, extensive retardation and hostility to adults. Over time, with care they formed attachments to carers and showed extensive physical and intellectual development, again demonstrating that privation effects, though severe, are reversible.

Evaluation of privation

● Case studies are used to study privation as other research methods would be unethical.

● The recoveries that the Czech twins and concentration camp survivors made may be explicable by the close attachments the children had to each other.

● Case studies are dependent upon retrospective memories that may be selective, incomplete or even dishonest, and as such can lack validity.

● Privation studies indicate that Bowlby's view of the negative effects of maternal deprivation being irreversible may be false.

● Privation research suggests that recovery is possible if a subsequent loving, nurturing relationship is encountered.

Examiner's tip

Studies of privation often take the form of case studies, therefore an effective way of evaluating such research could be through an assessment of the strengths and weaknesses of the case study method. This is best achieved by direct reference to a relevant study, such as the conflicting memories Genie's mother had of her daughter (Curtis 1977).

Now test yourself

9 Outline Bowlby's maternal deprivation hypothesis (MDH).

10 Is the maternal deprivation theory supported by research evidence?

11 Identify the components of distress caused by short-term deprivation.

12 What have research studies revealed about the effects of (i) short-term deprivation and (ii) long-term deprivation?

13 Why are institutionally reared children often regarded as examples of privation?

14 What have psychologists learned about the effects of privation?

Answers on p. 103

The impact of daycare

The term **daycare** refers to the temporary care of children outside the home provided by non-family members, for instance in nurseries, crèches and kindergartens. Daycare does not include institutional forms of childrearing like fostering and community homes or health-related forms of care like hospitalisation.

> **daycare** — temporary care of children by non-family members outside the family home

The care of children outside the family home raises passionate 'for' and 'against' arguments, making an unbiased, objective outlook difficult because political and religious opinions motivate people to find daycare beneficial or harmful instinctively. However, daycare is an economic necessity. In 2004, women with children under 5 years old comprised 52% of the British workforce.

Arguments for and against daycare

Revised

For daycare

- High quality daycare is stimulating, being run by motivated, well-trained practitioners. Activities not available at home and opportunities for interaction with other children are offered.

- Quality daycare has positive effects on social development; the negative effects of daycare are due to poor quality. Good quality daycare is associated with the sensitivity of carers to children in their care.

- Mothers who are free to work experience lower levels of stress, frustration and depression and interact and respond to children in more positive and healthy ways, making them better mothers.

Against daycare

- Separation from the primary caregiver results in deprivation leading to short-term and long-term damage to **social development**.

> **social development** — acquiring relationships with others and the social skills necessary within a cultural group

- Daycare is inferior to homecare as homecare offers a more loving and stimulating environment.

- Daycare brings negative outcomes; research evidence showing children raised at home incur superior social development.

Exam practice answers and quick quizzes at **www.therevisionbutton.co.uk/myrevisionnotes**

Aggression and peer relationships

Revised

Two areas of interest in the study of daycare have been its effect upon (1) children's aggression levels and (2) development of **peer relationships**.

peer relationships — associations with people of equal standing

Negative effects of daycare on aggression

Durkin (1995) reported that preschoolers who had been in daycare since infancy were prone to aggressiveness, negative social adjustment, hyperactivity and anxiety, compared with those starting daycare later, implying that the age children enter daycare is important.

A NICHD (2003) study found that children averaging 30 hours or more of childcare were more prone to problem behaviours, including aggressiveness, indicating that the amount of time in daycare is related to aggression levels.

Egeland & Hiester (1995) found securely, but not insecurely attached, children reacted aggressively to the extra attention that daycare incurs, implying that certain types of children are negatively affected by daycare.

Positive effects of daycare on aggression

Hagekull & Bohlin (1995) found that disadvantaged Swedish children, especially boys, receiving high-quality daycare showed reduced aggressiveness, suggesting that quality of daycare is important in lowering aggression.

A NICHD (2004) study using observations made by teachers and carers, rather than subjective ratings from mothers used in earlier studies, found children with high levels of daycare had lower levels of aggression, suggesting that daycare has a positive effect on aggressiveness.

Doherty (1996) found lower levels of aggression in children attending regular daycare, though high-quality care, low staff–children ratios, trained staff and stimulation were important factors.

Typical mistake

Many people have strong personal views on the desirability of putting children in daycare. Make sure any views you express on the topic are unbiased ones backed up by solid psychological facts and research. Examiners assess students on their knowledge of psychology, not their personal views and experiences however well they are expressed.

Evaluation of the effects of daycare on aggression

- Heightened levels of aggression may occur with daycare, because there is greater social interaction and more opportunity for aggression to arise.

- Family features, like quality of home environment, parental attitudes and maternal sensitivity, were better indicators of aggression levels and social development than quantity of daycare received. This suggests that quantity of daycare is not the most important factor in determining aggressiveness.

- Smith et al. (1998) believes aggressive behaviour is confused with rough-and-tumble play and therefore evidence of heightened aggression in daycare children is a misinterpretation of non-aggressive behaviour.

- Aggressive children are more likely to be put in daycare, as parents need a break, which suggests that factors other than daycare are responsible for the apparent heightened levels of aggression in daycare children.

Negative effects of daycare on peer relations

Guralnick et al. (1996) found that children with disabilities, like limited communication, motor and social skills, interact with peers less often and are less well accepted, suggesting that daycare is not beneficial for all children in developing peer relations.

2 Developmental psychology — early social development

Vliestra (1981) found that children attending half daycare had better peer relationships than those attending full daycare, implying that the amount of daycare is important in determining the quality of peer relationships.

Vandell & Corasaniti (1990) found that children receiving extensive daycare from untrained staff, with high staff–children ratios, developed inferior peer relations, implying that quality of daycare is related to quality of peer relationships.

Positive effects of daycare on peer relations

Clarke-Stewart et al. (1994) found that children with heightened ability to negotiate with peers were those receiving group-based daycare rather than homecare, suggesting that daycare helps to foster good peer relationships.

Rubenstein & Howes (1983) found that daycare encourages interactions with familiar peers, leading to a reduction in anxiety when meeting unfamiliar peers, implying daycare to have psychologically healthy outcomes.

Hartup & Moore (1990) found that daycare permits more extensive interactions with peers, teaches the rules of social interaction and helps resolve disputes with peers, implying that daycare is useful in achieving positive peer relationships.

Evaluation of the effects of daycare on peer relations

- Most research indicates that daycare permits greater opportunities for social contact and development of social skills, leading to positive peer relationships.

- It may harm the development of peer relations in children with low social competence and motor skills and provide opportunities for such children to be bullied by others.

- The development of good peer relations is dependent upon high-quality daycare provided by trained carers and low staff–children ratios. Evidence also suggests that too much daycare can negatively impact on peer relationships.

Evaluation of daycare research
Revised

- Evaluating daycare is not easy due to the huge variation in types and quality. Daycare research is also contaminated by bias. Belsky (2009) believes policy-makers should stop selectively embracing only the data consistent with their pre-existing viewpoints.

- High quality daycare, like that in Sweden, has positive developmental outcomes. However in many countries only the wealthy can afford such care and most children have lower quality care, with negative outcomes.

- Different methods of rating behaviour, like using teacher ratings rather than parental ratings, may lead to differences in findings, suggesting that differences in research findings are due to methodology.

- Top quality daycare is not related to quantity. Sensitivity of care is more important than the amount of time carers spend with children.

- Most research is correlational and does not show causality. Other variables may be involved, like working mums being stressed and contributing to elevated levels of aggressiveness in children.

Implications of research into daycare

Deprivation of maternal attachment through attending daycare was originally perceived as incurring serious, irreversible effects. However, research has identified factors, like high-quality daycare, which can benefit children's social development.

Implication of negative effects

Revised

Research suggests that attending daycare for long periods can negatively affect attachments. Belsky and Rovine (1988) found that 43% of babies in daycare for at least 4 months before their first birthday and for more than 20 hours per week, were likely to develop insecure attachments compared to 26% of 'home-reared' babies, while Violata and Russell's (1994) meta-analysis of 88 studies, found those receiving over 20 hours of daycare a week incurred negative effects on social development. This implies that young children should only attend daycare for short periods and policy-makers and employers should consider this when formulating the workloads of mothers returning to work.

Daycare is not beneficial to all. Pennebaker et al. (1981) found that shy children did not incur positive social development, while a NICHD study (1997) found that insecurely attached children did not develop well socially either. Research needs to identify which types of children are vulnerable to negative effects of daycare, so that assessments can occur, with those vulnerable being specially catered for. However such assessments would intrude into personal lives, like details of parents' background.

Borge et al.'s (2004) study found that daycare lowers aggressiveness in children from high-risk families. This was supported by Hagekull and Bohlin's (1995) finding that disadvantaged Swedish children receiving high quality daycare had reduced aggression levels, boys especially benefiting. Policy-makers should ensure such children are identified and receive high-quality daycare, as the benefits to society are worthwhile and cost-effective.

Research into childminding, like Mayall and Petrie (1977) and Bryant et al. (1980), found negative effects like insecure attachments and retarded development of language and cognitive skills. However such findings may be related to home circumstances because no control groups were used for comparison. Logically, if childminders were well trained and offered top-quality care they should be as beneficial as good-quality daycare.

> ### Examiner's tip
>
> In order to create effective answers on how research into attachment and daycare has influenced childcare practices it is advisable to have knowledge of what constitutes good and bad practice and to be able to refer to relevant research to back up your comments.

Implications of positive effects

Revised

Daycare can also benefit mothers as it offers respite from the stress of childcare and presents employment opportunities, bringing financial rewards and other benefits like increased self-esteem and lower levels

2 Developmental psychology — early social development

of depression. Unstressed mothers with elevated self-esteem can then interact with their children in more meaningful and constructive manners.

Mooney and Munton (1997), reviewing 40 years research, found no evidence of working mothers harming children's emotional or social development, while Rout et al. (1997) found that working mothers were superior to non-working mothers on levels of mental health, reporting less depression and stress. This shows the positive, rather than the negative effects of being a working mother.

As high-quality daycare has been shown to be beneficial, research has set out to identify the characteristics of high quality daycare (see Table 2.1), so that such features become routine features of daycare practices.

Table 2.1 The characteristics of high-quality daycare

Components	Description
Verbal interaction	Encouraging regular two-way communications between carers and children is stimulating and helps cement relationships
Stimulation	Good provision of toys, books, interaction etc
Sensitive emotional care	Use of carers sensitive and responsive to children's needs
Low staff turnover	Achieved by providing a good working environment, training and financial reward
Consistency of care	Having the same carers tending a child allows secure attachments to form
Low staff–children ratio	A staff to children ratio of about 3:1 is ideal, though this varies with age, smaller groups being easier for younger children to deal with
Mixed age groups	Groups comprised of younger and older children allows younger children opportunities to learn social behaviours through observation and imitation
Structured time	Activities should be structured as part of a routine, creating a predictable, calming environment, with some free play time available too

Providing high-quality daycare is expensive but cost-effective, as it incurs benefits to society such as helping develop worthy, constructive individuals of positive use to society, making huge savings in terms of social welfare costs, mental health care, etc.

As Clarke-Stewart (1989) says, 'maternal employment is a reality. The issue today, therefore, isn't whether infants should be in daycare but how to make their experiences there and at home supportive of their development and of their parents' peace of mind'.

Now test yourself

Tested

15 What is meant by daycare?
16 Outline the arguments for and against daycare.
17 What evaluative points can be made about the effects of daycare on aggression and peer relations?
18 Identify the components of good quality daycare.
19 What implications for childcare practices has research into attachment and daycare suggested?

Answers on p. 103

Exam practice

1 Outline the key features of Bowlby's theory of attachment. [6]
2 Explain two limitations of Bowlby's theory of attachment. [2 + 2]
3 Outline and evaluate the learning theory explanation of attachment. [12]
4 Outline the strange situation method of assessing attachment. [6]
5 To what extent has psychological research shown there are cultural variations in attachment. [6]
6 Two-year old Lachlan had a secure, loving relationship with his mother. While his mother was away visiting a sick relative, some psychologists observed Lachlan's reaction to having his attachment disrupted.

   (a) Outline two behavioural categories the psychologists could observe. [4]

   (b) Explain one strategy that could be used while Lachlan's mother was away to minimise possible negative effects of disrupting his attachment. [3]

7 Research has shown that there are negative effects to raising children in institutions. Hollie was placed in institutional care from birth, where there were no opportunities to form attachments, until she was adopted at age four.

   Outline some possible negative effects of institutional care on Hollie. [6]

Answers and quick quiz 2 online

Online

Examiner's summary

✔ Learning theory believes children develop attachments to feeders through conditioning processes; Bowlby saw attachment as an innate, evolved behaviour, enhancing survival, a view that better prepared candidates will show is more supported by research than learning theory.

✔ Ainsworth's development of the strange situation identified three basic attachment types: *secure*, *insecure–avoidant* and *insecure–resistant*. These should be known in terms of their characteristics and research supporting their existence.

✔ Use of the strange situation cross-culturally shows differences in attachment styles within and between cultures, though the strange situation is not applicable to all cultures.

✔ Bowlby's maternal deprivation hypothesis sees disrupted attachments as leading to serious, irreversible damage to children's development, though care should be taken not to confuse deprivation (referring to loss of attachment figures either in the short or long term) with privation (referring to attachment bonds never forming).

✔ Daycare was originally perceived as incurring negative effects upon maternal attachments, but research suggests that high-quality daycare benefits social development. Students should be able to present such research, identifying factors necessary for good childcare practices.

3 Research methods

The experimental method

Research methods are the means by which psychologists construct and test theories of the mind and behaviour. There are several research methods, each with strengths and limitations and each applicable in different circumstances.

The **experimental method** assigns participants randomly to conditions and manipulates variables to determine **causality**. An experimenter manipulates an **independent variable** (IV), for example the amount of sleep participants are allowed, to see its measured effect on the **dependent variable** (DV), such as speed of reaction to a flashing light. Therefore any change in the level of the DV occurs as a result of manipulating the IV, such as reaction times being slower with less sleep.

Experiments are conducted under **controlled conditions**, where researchers attempt to keep all variables (anything that can vary such as noise levels), apart from the IV, constant for all participants.

Extraneous variables are other variables that may affect the DV, such as noise levels, which if uncontrolled may become confounding variables and 'confuse' the results.

There are three main types of experiment: laboratory, field and natural.

> **research methods** — the means by which explanations are tested
>
> **experimental method** — research method using random assignment of participants and the manipulation of variables to determine cause and effect
>
> **causality** — cause and effect relationships
>
> **independent variable** — the factor manipulated by researchers in an investigation; the thing that differs between the conditions of an experiment
>
> **dependent variable** — the factor measured by researchers in an investigation, always a measurement of some sort

Laboratory experiments
Revised

When conducting a **laboratory experiment** the experimenter controls as many extraneous variables as possible, in a controlled environment (laboratory) using standardised procedures (procedural instructions that are same for all participants) and makes accurate, objective measurements.

> **laboratory experiment** — experiment conducted in a controlled environment allowing the establishment of causality

Strengths of laboratory experiments

- A high degree of control is maintained over variables, with the independent variable and dependent variable being precisely defined and measured, leading to greater accuracy and objectivity.
- They can be **replicated** (repeated exactly) to check the findings.
- As extraneous variables are controlled, causality is established (i.e. any change in the value of the DV is due to the manipulation of the IV).
- Individual pieces of behaviour can be isolated and rigorously tested.

Weaknesses of laboratory experiments

- Operationalising the independent and dependent variable so that accurate measurements can be made can involve them becoming

Exam practice answers and quick quizzes at **www.therevisionbutton.co.uk/myrevisionnotes**

over-specific and therefore not really related to actual behaviour, for example specifying a certain amount of weight increase rather than just 'getting fatter'.

- High levels of control can make experiments artificial and thus lacking in ecological validity (see page 47).
- Individual pieces of behaviour do not usually occur in isolation and laboratories can be intimidating environments, which again can induce non-normal reactions that are not representative of real life settings. Participants may behave how they feel the experimenter wants them to (**demand characteristics**) or in a way that deliberately sabotages the experiment (**screw-you-phenomenon**).

Field and natural experiments

Revised

Field experiments are similar to laboratory experiments in that an experimenter controls variables and manipulates an independent variable, but the study occurs in a 'real-world' setting and participants may be unaware they are taking part in an experiment.

In a **natural experiment** the independent variable occurs naturally (such as gender), with an experimenter merely measuring the effect on the dependent variable. This type of experiment can occur when it would be unethical to manipulate the IV (e.g. assessing the effects of abuse in families).

> **field experiment** — experiment conducted in a naturalistic setting where the investigator manipulates an independent variable
>
> **natural experiment** — experiment conducted in a naturalistic setting with a naturally occurring independent variable

Strengths of field and natural experiments

- Due to the 'real-world' scenario, participants' results relate more to real-life environments and behaviour and thus findings are more able to be generalised to other settings.
- Because participants are generally unaware that they are in an experiment they behave in a natural way and thus there are no demand characteristics.
- As they both contain objectively defined dependent variables, it is possible, as with laboratory experiments, to make accurate measurements of the effects of IVs upon DVs, demonstrating any differences between the experimental conditions.

Weaknesses of field and natural experiments

- It is more difficult to control extraneous variables, therefore there is less control over the experimental conditions and thus causality is harder to establish.
- As conditions will never be exactly the same again, it is difficult to replicate these types of experiments.
- There can be an ethical issue of a lack of informed consent, as participants may not be aware they are in an experiment. This applies more to field experiments because in natural experiments, with the IV occurring naturally, gaining consent may be unnecessary (as they are not actually experiments).
- As participants are not randomly allocated to conditions, there may be sample bias that 'confuses' the results.

> **Examiner's tip**
>
> An easy criticism to remember about natural experiments that could be used as an example of a weakness of the technique is that due to the lack of manipulation/control over an independent variable, they are not really experiments at all. Indeed they are often referred to as 'quasi- (semi) experiments' as it is not possible to allocate participants to conditions randomly.

Correlations

Correlational studies

Positive **correlations** occur where co-variables increase together, for example as the temperature rises, ice-cream sales also rise. A negative correlation occurs where as one co-variable increases, another decreases, for example as the temperature increases, umbrella sales decrease.

> **correlations** — investigations that measure the degree of relationship between co-variables

A correlation co-efficient is a numerical value, ranging from +1.0 (perfect positive correlation) to -1.0 (perfect negative correlation), displaying the degree to which co-variables are related.

Strengths of correlations

● Correlations can be used where manipulation of variables would be difficult or unethical.

● Once a correlation is found, predictions can be made, for example predicting the number of ice-creams sold on hot days.

● Correlations show the strength and direction of relationships and can identify patterns among variables to inform subsequent experimentation.

Weaknesses of correlations

● Correlations are not conducted under controlled conditions and therefore do not show causality, making interpretation of results difficult.

● Seemingly low correlations (e.g. +0.14) can actually be significant if the number of recorded scores is high. Conversely, apparently high correlations (e.g. +0.69) can be insignificant if the number of recorded scores is low.

● Other non-measured extraneous variables can influence the measured co-variables, again making interpretation of results difficult.

Observations

Naturalistic observations

Naturalistic observations generally measure naturally occurring behaviour in the real world, such as hooliganism at football matches, although they can also occur under controlled conditions as a laboratory study (e.g. Milgram).

> **naturalistic observations** — surveillance and recording of naturally occurring events

Naturalistic observations should only occur in circumstances where people would expect to be involved. Observations can be (a) **participant**, where observers are actively involved in the behaviour of those being studied, or (b) **non-participant**, where observers are not actively involved in the behaviour of those being studied. Observations can also be either

Exam practice answers and quick quizzes at **www.therevisionbutton.co.uk/myrevisionnotes**

(i) **overt**, with participants aware they are being studied or (ii) **covert**, with participants unaware they are being studied.

To produce **reliable** (consistent) results, which are free from **observer bias** (seeing what they want to see), **inter-rater reliability** must be established.

> **inter-rater reliability** — where observers' observations are correlated (checked) against each other to ensure that they are observing in the same, consistent way (e.g. that two independent observers categorise children's play in the same way)

Strengths of observations

- As they occur in the real world with participants behaving naturally, they have high **external validity**, meaning that results can be generalised to other settings.

- They can be used where deliberate manipulations of variables would be impractical or unethical, where co-operation from those being studied is unlikely, where the full social context of behaviour is required and where animals or children are being studied.

- As participants are often unaware of being studied, **demand characteristics** are reduced (see page 49).

Weaknesses of observations

- Ethical issues of **invasion of privacy** and **informed consent** arise where participants are unaware of being studied. If participants are aware of being studied, then demand characteristics can occur.

- They are difficult to replicate as the lack of control over variables makes testing conditions difficult to repeat exactly.

- Practical problems can occur where it is difficult (a) for observers to remain undetected, (b) to observe and record all behaviour, and (c) to categorise observed behaviours correctly.

> **Typical mistake**
>
> Students are often confused by different terms that mean the same thing. For instance, *inter-rater, inter-coder* and *inter-observer reliability* all essentially mean that different observers agree upon and categorise behaviours in the same way. The more you familiarise yourself with psychological terminology, the fewer such confusions will occur.

Self-reports

Self-reports are research methods where participants generate data about themselves, such as by using questionnaires and interviews.

> **self-reports** — investigations where participants give information about themselves without researcher interference

Questionnaires
Revised ☐

Questionnaires are a written method of data collection concerning behaviour, opinions and attitudes. Two main types of question are used: (1) **closed questions**, where response options are fixed by the researchers (e.g. yes/no tick boxes) which are easy to quantify, but restrict answers; (2) **open questions**, where participants respond in their own words, where responses are harder to quantify, but allow greater freedom of expression.

> **questionnaires** — self-report method where respondents give written answers to pre-set questions

Strengths of questionnaires

- Compared to other methods, large amounts of information can be collected in a relatively short space of time.

- As standardised questions are used they are easy to replicate, especially the closed questions.

- Researchers are not required to be present and can therefore generate large samples.

Weaknesses of questionnaires

- Participants may give **socially desirable** or **idealised** answers (where they answer in terms of how society would expect them to answer, or how they would like to be).
- Designing questionnaires is difficult; participants can easily misunderstand or misinterpret questions.
- They are uneconomical; they incur low response rates and are often biased and unrepresentative as certain types of people are more willing to complete them.

Interviews

Revised

Interviews involve interviewers asking participants questions verbally. With **structured** (formal) interviews, identical, quantitative questions (those that produce numerical data) are read to participants and interviewers simply record answers. **Unstructured** (informal) interviews involve less controlled, informal discussion of pre-determined topics allowing further investigation of interesting responses. Interviewers in unstructured interviews require the skill to establish friendly relationships, enabling them to gain significant levels of detail and understanding. Mainly qualitative data (non-numerical) is produced.

Semi-structured interviews combine structured and unstructured techniques, to produce quantitative and qualitative data.

interviews — self-report method where respondents give verbal answers to questions in face-to-face situations

Strengths of interviews

- Complicated and/or sensitive issues, like sexuality, can be explored, especially in unstructured interviews.
- The variety and flexibility of interview techniques permits the generation and analysis of both quantitative and qualitative data.
- Ambiguities and misunderstandings can be clarified. Unstructured interviews allow interesting follow-up questions to be asked and questions can be especially adapted to the circumstances of individual participants.

Examiner's tip

An essential way of earning all the marks available for an examination question is to elaborate answers with relevant detail. So, for example, when studying interviews ensure that you are able to outline the differences between the different sub-types, such as between structured and unstructured interviews. This strategy can equally be used other topic areas.

Weaknesses of interviews

- Interviewers can unconsciously bias respondents' answers through their appearance, attitude, gender etc.
- Much skill and training is required to conduct unstructured interviews, especially into sensitive issues. Such highly trained interviewers are not easy to come by.
- Ethical issues arise when interviewees are not aware of the true purpose of interviews and respondents may reveal more than they wish, incurring an invasion of privacy.

Exam practice answers and quick quizzes at **www.therevisionbutton.co.uk/myrevisionnotes**

Case studies

Case studies Revised

Case studies are in-depth investigations usually including detailed biographical and behavioural details. Individual past histories are explored to reveal insights into current situations, using material from individuals themselves and those close to them. Other research methods, like interviews, are often made use of, if they seem relevant.

> **case studies** — in-depth investigations of one individual or small group

Strengths of case studies

- Rich detail and understanding of an individual can emerge rather than an average gathered from many.

- They are useful for theory falsification, which can be achieved with just one contradictory example.

- They allow exploration of behaviours/experiences so unique that they cannot be investigated by other means, especially sensitive/unethical areas like sexual abuse.

Weaknesses of case studies

> **false memory syndrome** — where participants recall untrue 'suggested' events
>
> **researcher bias** — where subjective interpretation of data occurs, making results non-objective and thus non-factual

- They are unrepresentative, meaning findings cannot be generalised to others.

- They often rely on participants having full and accurate memories; **false memory syndrome** can occur.

- The study method is prone to **researcher bias**.

Now test yourself Tested

1. What is meant by (i) an independent variable (IV)? (ii) a dependent variable (DV)?
2. What are controlled conditions?
3. Explain what extraneous variables are and how they may become confounding variables.
4. Describe the following types of experiments, highlighting the differences between them: (i) laboratory (ii) field (iii) natural.
5. What do correlations measure?
6. Explain the difference between a positive and a negative correlation.
7. Describe observational studies, including participant/non-participant observations and overt/covert observations.
8. What is meant by inter-rater reliability? Explain how it is established.
9. What are questionnaires?
10. Explain the difference between open and closed questions in questionnaires.
11. What are interviews? Highlight the differences between (i) structured (ii) unstructured and (iii) semi-structured interviews.
12. Describe the case study research method.

Answers on p. 104

Aims and hypotheses

Aims

An **aim** is a question(s), generated by previous research or observations, that a study is designed to answer (e.g. to study the effects of caffeine on reaction times).

> **aim** — precise statement of why investigations are occurring

Hypotheses

Hypotheses are research predictions, occurring as two types.

> **hypotheses** — precise, testable research predictions

1 **The experimental (alternative) hypothesis** — predicts a difference in the dependent variable (the variable being measured) as a result of manipulation of the independent variable which is significant (beyond the boundaries of chance). There are two types of experimental/alternative hypotheses: (a) **one-tailed** (directional) which predicts not only a difference in levels of the DV but in which direction the difference will lie (e.g. 'women will score higher on IQ than men'); and (b) **two-tailed** (non-directional) which predicts a difference, but not the direction in which it will go (e.g. 'there will be a difference in men and women's IQ scores'). One-tailed hypotheses are used when previous research indicates which direction results will lie in and two-tailed hypotheses are used in new research areas, or where previous research results are contradictory.

2 **The null hypothesis** — predicts that manipulation of the IV will not affect the DV, any differences witnessed being a result of chance factors (e.g. 'there will be no difference between women's and men's IQ scores').

Either the experimental or the null hypothesis will be supported by findings, allowing one to be accepted and one rejected.

> **Typical mistake**
>
> You may get asked to compose an aim or a hypothesis in an examination question; many students confuse the two and thus lose marks. Quite simply an aim is a *statement about what is being investigated* (e.g. the effects of audiences on athletic performance), while a hypothesis is a *prediction of what will occur* (e.g. that participants will perform better with an audience than without).

Experimental design

There are three main types of experimental design: (1) independent groups design (IGD) (2) repeated measures design (RMD) and (3) matched participants. Each has strengths and weaknesses.

Independent groups

In an **independent groups design** each experimental condition is made up of participants who are independent of each other (e.g. running a timed 400 metres either with or without an audience).

> **independent groups design** — experimental design in which each participant performs only one condition of an experiment

Strengths of independent groups design

- As participants each do only one condition of the experiment, demand characteristics are reduced as there is less chance that participants will guess the aim of the study.

- As different participants are used in each condition there are no order effects (see *weaknesses of repeated measures design* below).

Weaknesses of independent groups design

- Participants only generate one piece of data each, half that of participants in a repeated measures design, meaning that twice as many participants are required.
- Differences in findings between conditions may actually be due to **participant variables** (differences between individual participants), such as natural differences in running ability, rather than manipulations of the independent variable. This can be reduced by randomly allocating participants to conditions to balance out differences, thus making each testing group similar in composition.

Examiner's tip

A useful method of learning the strengths and weaknesses of the independent groups design and repeated measures design is to remember that the strengths of one are the weaknesses of the other. For instance, a weakness of the RMD is that there are order effects but a strength of the IGD is its lack of order effects.

Repeated measures
Revised

Each participant in a **repeated measures design** is being tested against themselves rather than a different participant as in IGD (e.g. running a timed 400 metres with and without an audience).

Strengths of repeated measures design

- As each participant does all conditions, there are no participant variables.
- Participants generate twice as much individual data as in an independent group design, meaning that half the number of participants are needed.

Weaknesses of repeated measures design

- As each participant does all conditions, **order effects** may occur. Order effects can be addressed by **counterbalancing**, where half the participants do one condition first (e.g. run with an audience), and half the other condition first e.g. run without an audience.
- As participants do all conditions, demand characteristics are more likely through guessing the aims of the study and performing as they believe they are expected to.

repeated measures design — experimental design where participants perform all conditions of an experiment

order effects — the order in which conditions are done can affect results (e.g. participants may perform worse in the second condition due to tiredness, or perform better due to a practice/ learning effect)

Matched participants design
Revised

Matched participants design is a special kind of repeated measures design, where different but similar participants are used in each experimental condition. Participants are pre-tested on relevant variables and then matched into similar pairs (e.g. in terms of running ability). MZ (identical) twins are often used as, being genetically identical, they form perfect matched pairs.

matched participants design — experimental design where participants are in similar pairs, with one of each pair performing each condition

Strengths of matched participants design

- As different participants do each condition, there are no order effects and less chance of demand characteristics.
- As participants are matched, there are fewer participant variables than with an independent groups design.

Weaknesses of matched participants design

- Achieving matched pairs by pre-testing can be a lengthy process.
- It is almost impossible to match participants on all important variables, plus at any given moment even matched participants will differ in terms of motivation and energy levels.

Designing observations

Revised

Target behaviours are divided into separate **behavioural categories** agreed before observations occur. Behaviours are often coded/rated on previously agreed scales and recorded onto a grid/coding sheet for later analysis.

Standardisation between observers/raters is checked before observations occur to ensure inter-rater reliability (that raters are agreed on behavioural categories and are recording and rating data identically).

> **behavioural categories** — target behaviours divided into sub-sets through use of coding systems (e.g. different types of children's play like solo play, make believe play)

Designing self-reports

Revised

There are five important factors to consider when designing questionnaires in order to get a reasonable response rate: (1) only ask relevant questions, (2) keep them short as over-long questionnaires will not be completed, (3) use successful questionnaires as a guide, (4) ask clear, concise and easily understood questions, and (5) initial questions should be interesting to motivate people to complete.

Some questionnaires use a measuring scale, like the **Likert scale**, which measures both direction and strength of attitudes. For example:

Rate your level of agreement with the following statement:

'Schools should provide nutritious, healthy meals for free'

1	2	3	4	5
Strongly agree	*Agree*	*Undecided*	*Disagree*	*Strongly disagree*

With interviews, decisions about type of interviewer and choices of important interpersonal variables (e.g. gender, ethnicity, personal characteristics) must be made.

Interviewer training is an essential factor in successful interviewing; interviewers need to know when to (and not to) speak and how to use non-verbal communication to ease participants into giving full and honest answers.

> **Typical mistake**
>
> Students are often confused about experimental methods and designs and talk about the wrong ones when answering examination questions. Quite simply, **experimental methods** refer to *laboratory, field and natural* experiments, while **experimental designs** refer to *independent groups, repeated measures and matched participants* designs.

Variables and controls

Operationalisation of variables

Revised

Operationalisation involves defining variables simply and objectively in order to manipulate them (independent variables) and measure them

> **operationalisation** — defining variables into measurable factors

(dependent variables). For instance, if investigating the influence of caffeine consumption on reaction times, the IV could be operationalised as the amount of caffeine drunk and the DV as speed of reaction to a buzzer.

Pilot studies

Revised

Pilot studies allow investigators to check and make appropriate changes to the research design, method and analysis, thus improving the quality of the research and avoiding having to repeat the research due to unforeseen errors. These studies give an indication of whether meaningful results may be found, thus indicating whether planned research on a larger scale is worth undertaking.

> **pilot studies** — small-scale practice investigations

Control of extraneous variables

Revised

In experiments, researchers wish to see the effect of manipulating an independent variable upon a dependent variable. Other variables that affect a DV are known as **extraneous variables**. Researchers need to control these across the different experimental conditions. Uncontrolled extraneous variables that confuse results are known as **confounding variables**.

> **extraneous variables** — variables other than the manipulation of an independent variable that cause changes in the level of a dependent variable

There are three main areas where extraneous variables arise:
(1) **participant variables**, such as participants' ages and intelligence levels, (2) **situational variables** (the experimental environment), like temperature and noise levels, and (3) **experimenter variables**, where changes in the researcher's appearance and behaviour can affect the findings (e.g. female researchers may elicit different participant behaviour than male researchers).

Reliability and validity

Revised

Results that show **reliability** are **consistent** (i.e. an exactly repeated study produces identical findings). Results that show **validity** are **accurate** (i.e. a precise measure of what they claim to measure).

Reliable results are not necessarily valid (e.g. finding on several occasions that 1+1=3 is a reliable result but not a valid one).

Internal reliability is when a test is consistent within itself (e.g. a set of scales weighing the same weight between 0–50 grams, as between 100–150 grams). **External reliability** is assessed by the **test–re-test** method and is when a test produces consistent results over time.

Internal validity is when results occur due to manipulation of an independent variable and not confounding variables. For IV to occur requires no **investigator effects** (see page 49), no demand characteristics, use of **standardised instructions** (identical instructions given to all participants) and use of **random samples** (see page 49). **External (ecological) validity** is where results can be generalised beyond the experimental setting (e.g. to different populations, settings and time eras). Field and natural experiments, plus naturalistic observations, usually have high external validity.

> **Typical mistake**
>
> Students often misinterpret questions. For instance, a question may ask for an *explanation* of a confounding variable, but instead an *example* is supplied (or an explanation is given when an example is called for). Therefore always read the question carefully and then re-read your response to ensure it actually answers the question asked.

> **reliability** — the extent to which a test or measure produces consistent results
>
> **validity** — the extent to which findings accurately measure what they claim to measure

Ethical issues

Ethical guidelines

Ethical issues must be fully considered before research occurs by adherence to **ethical guidelines** published by the British Psychological Society (BPS) and by reference to ethical committees of relevant research institutions.

ethical guidelines — the rules governing the conduct of researchers in investigations

Informed consent — participants should be given sufficient prior details of research that enables them to make a considered decision as to whether they wish to participate. Additional parental consent is required for those under the age of 16.

Avoidance of deception — withholding information and misleading participants should be avoided. There are ways of dealing with unavoidable deception in order not to reveal a hypothesis:
(a) **presumptive consent** — gaining informed consent from those similar to the actual participants, (b) **prior general consent** — gaining the consent of participants to be deceived without them knowing how this will occur.

Examiner's tip

Examination questions often ask about ethical issues, as well as strategies to deal with them. A good way of studying this area is to learn individual ethical issues and what they mean, coupled with strategies for dealing with them. Learning relevant examples from research studies can also provide valuable extra detail.

Right to withdraw — participants are informed they can leave a study at any time, including withdrawing their data at the conclusion of a study. Providing the right to withdraw is a means of retrospectively dealing with deception.

Briefing/debriefing — full relevant details should be explained before and after a study is conducted. Debriefing can help to deal with deception and eliminate harm by ensuring participants leave studies in the same state they entered them.

Protection of participants — participants must be protected from physical and mental harm. Risk of harm must be no greater than in real life.

Confidentiality — data is not disclosed to others/used for other purposes unless agreed in advance. Numbers should be used instead of names in published research.

Observations — observations should only be made in settings where people would expect to be observed.

Cost-benefit analysis — if the potential benefits of research (e.g. the knowledge gained) are deemed to outweigh possible negative ethical implications (e.g. distress caused) then research may be considered ethically acceptable.

Sampling

A population is all of something (e.g. all the students in the 6th form), while a sample is a part of a population, which ideally should be representative (possessing the same characteristics of the sample from which it is drawn). **Target populations** are the groups of people to whom researchers aim to generalise their results.

Several **sampling** methods exist, each with strengths and weaknesses.

1 **Random sampling** occurs where every member of a population has an equal chance of being selected (e.g. names out of a hat). Random samples are generally representative, but this is not guaranteed, for instance all females could be selected. Not all members of a population may be available for selection.

2 **Opportunity sampling** involves selecting those available and willing to take part. Although convenient, this sample can be unrepresentative (e.g. all shoppers).

3 **Self-selected (volunteer) sampling** involves using those who select themselves, often by replying to advertisements. Volunteers are usually keen, but can be unrepresentative and prone to demand characteristics.

> **sampling** — the selection of participants to represent a wider population

> **Typical mistake**
>
> A very common mistaken belief is that random sampling guarantees a representative sample. Random sampling could theoretically select a sample of all one type of person, which is very unrepresentative.

Demand characteristics   Revised ☐

Demand characteristics can involve (1) participants unconsciously guessing the purpose of research and attempting to give the 'desired' behaviour/results, (2) the '*screw-you effect*', where participants guess the purpose of the research and attempt to give a false result, (3) acting unnaturally out of nervousness/fear of evaluation, and (4) acting unnaturally by giving socially desirable answers (see page 42).

> **demand characteristics** — a research effect where participants form impressions of the aim(s) and alter their behaviour accordingly

The **single blind procedure** is a technique that can reduce demand characteristics by not allowing participants knowledge of which condition they are in (e.g. not knowing in a drug trial if they have been given a real drug or a placebo — a harmless dummy pill).

Investigator effects   Revised ☐

Investigators can accidentally influence results in several ways.

1 **Primary physical characteristics** — certain obvious physical aspects of investigators can affect findings (e.g. age, ethnicity).

2 **Secondary physical characteristics** — certain less obvious physical aspects can also affect findings (e.g. accent, degree of eye-contact) giving hints as how to behave, which leads to demand characteristics.

3 **Bias** — investigators may inadvertently be biased in their interpretation of data.

The **double-blind procedure** is a technique that can reduce investigator effects; neither participants nor investigators know which condition participants are in, so that unconscious clues as how to behave are not transmitted.

> **investigator effects** — researcher features that influence participants' responses

Now test yourself

13 What is the purpose of an aim in a psychological investigation?

14 What is a hypothesis?

15 Outline the differences between the following experimental designs: (i) independent groups design (IGD) (ii) repeated measures design (RMD) (iii) matched participants design (MPD).

16 What factors should be included in the design of questionnaires to encourage a reasonable response rate?

17 What factors need to be considered to conduct a successful interview?

18 Explain the term operationalisation.

19 Explain what pilot studies are. Why they are conducted?

20 In terms of ethical considerations, explain how researchers can: (i) obtain informed consent (ii) avoid deception (iii) debrief participants (iv) protect participants from harm (v) ensure the right to withdraw (vi) establish confidentiality (vii) conduct observations in an ethical manner.

21 Explain the following terms and give a limitation of each: (i) random sampling (ii) opportunity sampling (iii) self-selected sampling.

22 What are demand characteristics? How can they be reduced?

23 In what ways can investigator effects influence results? How can they be reduced?

Answers on p. 104

Quantitative data

All research generates data, which need to be presented, analysed and interpreted in ways that promote objective, meaningful understanding and thus advance knowledge. Data can either be **quantitative** (occurring in numerical form), or **qualitative** (occurring in descriptive form).

Quantitative data are objective, precise, reliable and numerical in nature and, although lacking in the detail of qualitative data, can be presented in a variety of ways to draw out a depth of meaning.

> **quantitative data** — are objective, reliable and numerical (e.g. in graphs, tables, measures of central tendency and dispersion)

Graphs

Graphs allow quantitative data to be presented in visually meaningful ways and can help to draw out data patterns.

> **graphs** — easily understandable visual presentations of numerical data

Graphs require an appropriate title and accurate labels for each axis that identify units of measurement used. Only one type of graph should be used to illustrate a set of data (i.e., the most appropriate).

Different types of graphs exist for different types of research data:

1 Bar charts

Bar charts show data in the form of categories that researchers wish to compare (see Figure 3.1). Categories are placed on the horizontal x-axis (e.g. males and females). The columns of bar charts should be of equal width and separated by spaces to indicate that the variable on the x-axis is not continuous.

Data are 'discrete', such as the mean score of several groups, but can also involve percentages, ratios and totals. A bar chart can display two values together.

Exam practice answers and quick quizzes at **www.therevisionbutton.co.uk/myrevisionnotes**

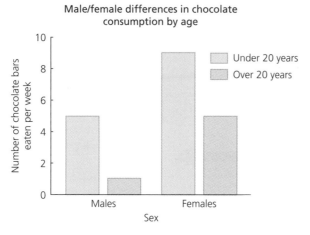

Figure 3.1 Example of a bar chart

2 Histograms

Histograms are used for continuous data, like test scores/values, which increase along the horizontal x-axis, while the frequency of the values is shown on the vertical y-axis (see Figure 3.2). There are no spaces between the columns (unlike bar charts) as data is continuous. The columns for each value on the x-axis should be of equal width.

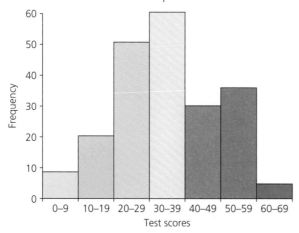

Figure 3.2 Example of a histogram

3 Frequency polygons (line graphs)

Similar to a histogram, in that the data on the horizontal x-axes are continuous, a frequency polygon is created by drawing a line from the mid-point top of each bar in a histogram. Frequency polygons allow two or more frequency distributions to be compared on the same graph (see Figure 3.3).

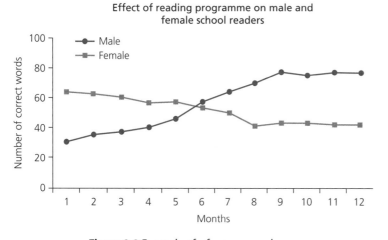

Figure 3.3 Example of a frequency polygon

4 Scattergrams (scattergraphs)

Scattergrams are used for correlational data (see page 40), showing the extent to which co-variables are related. One co-variable is represented on the horizontal x-axis and another co-variable on the vertical y-axis. Positive correlations are shown by data sloping upwards from left to right. Negative correlations are shown by data sloping downwards from left to right (see Figure 3.4).

Examiner's tip

You will not be asked to draw a graph in your examination but there is a possibility you could be asked to interpret one. Therefore it is essential that you study graphs to learn the different types, under what circumstances you would use them and what their features mean.

–0.9 –0.9 –0.8 –0.7 –0.6 –0.5 –0.4 –0.3 –0.1 –0.1 0 +0.1 +0.2 +0.3 +0.4 +0.5 +0.6 +0.7 +0.8 +0.9 +1

| perfect negative correlation | strong negative correlation | weak negative correlation | no correlation | weak positive correlation | strong positive correlation | perfect positive correlation |

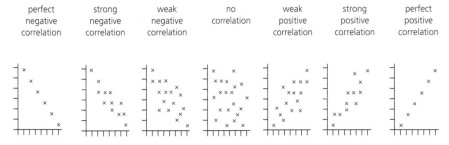

Figure 3.4 Scattergrams showing different types of correlations

Tables

Revised

Tables are another means of visually summarising numerical data in an easily understandable manner and again help to draw out patterns in data. Tables require a title and clear and accurate labels for each column, describing the units of measurement (see Table 3.1). When relevant, measure of central tendency, totals, percentages and measures of dispersion should be included within a table.

Table 3.1 The effect of an audience on running times over 200 metres

	Without audience	**With audience**
Total time in seconds	800	735
Mean time in seconds	40	35
Number of participants	20	21
Range of times in seconds	25	20

Measures of central tendency

Revised

There are three **measures of central tendency**: the **median**, the **mean** and the **mode**.

The median

The median is the middle score in a list of rank ordered scores (or the mid-point between the two middle scores with an even set of data). For example in the set of data 2,4,7,8,9 the median is 7 and in the set of data 3,4,6,7,7,9 the median is 6.5.

Strengths of the median

● It is not affected by extreme scores.

● It can be used with **ordinal** scores (the data can be put in rank order).

measures of central tendency — methods of estimating mid-point scores in sets of data by summarising large amounts of data into 'typical' scores

Weaknesses of the median

- It is not as sensitive as the mean, as not all the scores are used.
- It can be unrepresentative in a small set of data.

The mean

The mean is calculated by adding up all the scores and dividing by the number of scores to achieve a mid-point of the combined values. For example in the set of data 2, 7, 4, 8, 1, 3, 3, the mean is 4.

Strengths of the mean

- It makes use of all the scores in a set of data in its calculation.
- It is the most accurate measure of central tendency as it uses the **interval** level of measurement where the units of measurement are of equal size (e.g. seconds in time).

Weaknesses of the mean

- The mean score may not actually be one of the scores in the data.
- It can become **skewed** (unrepresentative) if there are extreme scores.

The mode

The mode is the most commonly occurring score in a set of data. For example in the set of data 2, 4, 5, 4, 7, 4, 2, 6, 4, the mode is 4.

Strengths of the mode

- It is less prone to distortion by extreme scores.
- It can make more sense than other measures of central tendency, for instance the average number of children in a British family is better described as 2 children (the mode) than 2.4 children (the mean).

Weaknesses of the mode

- More than one mode can occur in a set of data.
- It does not use all the scores.

Measures of dispersion
Revised

Measures of dispersion include the **range**, the **interquartile range** and **standard deviation**.

> **measures of dispersion** — measurements of the variability or spread of scores within a set of data

The range

The range is calculated by subtracting the lowest score from the highest score in a set of data. For example in the set of data 7, 2, 5, 6, 4, the range is 7-2=5.

Strengths of the range

- It is relatively easy and quick to calculate.
- It takes full account of extreme values.

Weaknesses of the range

- It can be distorted by extreme scores.
- It does not show if data are clustered or spread evenly around the mean.

The interquartile range

The interquartile range displays the spread of the middle 50% of data in a set of scores, for example 1, 3, **4**, **4**, **5**, **7**, 8, 8.

The upper limit in the interquartile range is the mean of the highest score in the middle 50% of data in a set of scores and the next score up (e.g. 7+8 (=15) ÷2 = 7.5).

The lower limit in the interquartile range is the mean of the lowest score in the middle 50% of data in a set of scores and the next score down (e.g. 4+3 (=7) ÷2 = 3.5).

The interquartile range is the difference between the upper and lower limits (e.g. 7.5 − 3.5 = 4).

Strengths of the interquartile range

- It is fairly easy to calculate.
- It is not affected by extreme scores.

Weaknesses of the interquartile range

- It does not make use of all the scores in a set of data.
- It becomes inaccurate if there are large intervals between individual scores.

Standard deviation

Standard deviation (SD) is a measure of the variability (spread) of a set of scores from the mean: the larger the SD, the larger the spread of scores.

To calculate SD: (i) calculate the mean, (ii) subtract the mean from each individual score, (iii) square each of these scores, (iv) add squared scores together, (v) calculate the variance by dividing the sum of the squares by the number of scores minus 1, and (vi) calculate SD by finding the square root of the variance.

Strengths of standard deviation

- It has sensitivity as all scores in a set of data are used.
- It allows for the interpretation of individual scores.

Weaknesses of standard deviation

- It is relatively complicated to calculate.
- It becomes less meaningful if data are not **normally distributed** (spread equally either side of a mean, with declining amounts of scores away from the mean).

Qualitative data

Qualitative data are often useful when investigating attitudes, opinions and beliefs. They can occur as verbal, written or pictorial descriptions. Although not as objective or easy to analyse as quantitative data, qualitative data convey detailed insight into the depth and range of human experience, which data reduced to numerical form can never do.

> **qualitative data** — non-numerical data that express meanings, feelings and descriptions (e.g. different types of children's drawings of a Christmas tree and presents)

Content analysis

Content analysis converts qualitative data into quantitative data, allowing the numerical analysis of written, verbal and visual communications, such as speeches, newspaper/magazine articles, drawings and advertisements.

Content analysis requires the creation of quantifiable coding units to categorise material to be analysed (e.g. counting the number of times women advertise attractiveness in 'lonely hearts' advertisements). Categorising through coding units can involve words, themes, characters or time and space.

Once qualitative data has been converted into quantitative data, it can be further analysed through the use of graphs, tables and statistical tests.

> **content analysis** — a method of quantifying qualitative data through the use of coding units (e.g. analysing the content of 'lonely hearts' advertisements to investigate whether men and women look for different things in relationships)

Now test yourself

24 Explain the difference between quantitative and qualitative data.

25 What do the following display: (i) bar charts (ii) histograms (iii) frequency polygons (iv) scattergrams?

26 Explain the following measures of central tendency: (i) median (ii) mean (iii) mode.

27 What do the following measures of dispersion show: (i) range (ii) interquartile range (iii) standard deviation?

28 Explain (i) what content analysis is and (ii) how it is conducted.

Answers on p. 104

Exam practice

1 A researcher, noting that previous research has indicated that excessive hours of daycare can have a negative impact upon social development of children, decides to carry out a study in this research area. A sample of 4-year-old children attending a day nursery for over 30 hours a week, was compared with a similar sample of 4 year olds attending the same nursery for less than 15 hours a week. Social development was measured on a social development index.

  (a) (i) Identify the independent variable in the study. [1]

     (ii) Identify the dependent variable in the study. [1]

  (b) (i) Select from the following options what kind of experimental design was used. [1]

       A matched participants design

       B repeated measures design

       C independent groups design

     (ii) Outline one strength and one weakness of this experimental design. [2 + 2]

  (c) (i) Compose a suitable one-tailed (directional) hypothesis for the study. [2]

     (ii) With reference to the study, explain why a one-tailed (directional) hypothesis would be suitable. [2]

  (d) Identify one possible extraneous variable in the study and explain what measures might be taken to stop it becoming a confounding variable. [1 + 2]

  (e) Before commencing the research the psychologist conducted a pilot study.

     (i) Explain what is meant by a pilot study. [2]

     (ii) Give two reasons why a pilot study might be carried out. [2 + 2]

  (f) The study was carried out as an experiment. Describe how the study could be carried out as a correlational analysis (your description could make reference to features such as the aim, the procedure, a correlational hypothesis, analysis of data etc). [10]

2 Ainsworth carried out research into infants' attachment types using the strange situation testing method. One possible ethical issue with this study method is protection of participants from harm.

(a) Explain two ways in which psychologists could deal with this issue. [2 + 2]

(b) (i) Outline another ethical issue that arises with the strange situation testing method. [2]

(ii) Explain one strategy that could be used to deal with this ethical issue. [2]

(c) Explain how a cost-benefit analysis can be used to assess whether research is ethical. [4]

Answers and quick quiz 3 online

Online

Examiner's summary

✔ Psychology uses several experimental and non-experimental research methods, each applicable in different circumstances. Students gaining better marks will be those who know individual methods in specific detail and demonstrate the ability to evaluate them in terms of their advantages and weaknesses.

✔ In order to maximise marks, familiarity is required with the individual features of investigation design. The best means of achieving this is to relate such features to actual research studies covered during the course.

✔ Both quantitative and qualitative data require presentation and analysis. While students are not required to create graphs, make calculations etc. in the examination they are expected to interpret and make informed comment upon examples of data presentation and to show knowledge of the circumstances in which they would be used.

Exam practice answers and quick quizzes at **www.therevisionbutton.co.uk/myrevisionnotes**

4 Biological psychology — stress

The body's response to stress

The two general bodily responses to **stress** are (1) the **sympatho-medullary pathway** (SMP) dealing with acute (short-term) stressors, and (ii) the **pituitary adrenal system** (PAS) dealing with chronic (long-term) **stressors**.

> **pituitary adrenal system** — bodily system responding to long-term, chronic stressors, comprised of the hypothalamus, the pituitary and adrenal glands

The sympatho-medullary pathway   Revised ☐

The sympatho-medullary pathway is made up of the **sympathetic nervous system** (SNS) and the **sympathetic adrenal medullary system** (SAM).

Acute stressors activate the two divisions of the **autonomic nervous system** (ANS):

1 the 'trouble-shooting' SNS, which responds to stressors and is responsible for emotional states and heightened arousal;

2 the 'housekeeping' **parasympathetic nervous system** (PNS) which maintains equilibrium and calms bodily processes.

When exposed to acute stressors the SNS is activated, while the SAM stimulates the release of noradrenaline from the adrenal glands in the adrenal medulla, thus preparing the body for 'flight or fight' by increasing oxygen and glucose supplies to the brain and muscles, while suppressing non-essential processes like digestion.

> **stress** — lack of balance between the perceived demands of a situation and perceived abilities to cope with such demands
>
> **stressors** — internal and external sources of stress
>
> **sympatho-medullary pathway** — bodily system responding to acute, short-term stressors, comprised of the sympathetic nervous system and the sympathetic adrenal medullary system

> **Horwatt et al. (1988)** exposed animals to the same stressor every day, finding that adaptive changes occurred in the sympatho-medullary pathway including the increased production of catecholamines ('flight or fight' hormones). When these animals were exposed to a new stressor, they demonstrated a heightened SMP response, suggesting that acute stress responses develop differently due to previous stress experiences.
>
> **Taylor et al. (2000)** found that acute stress produces the 'flight or fight' response in men but the 'tend and befriend' response in women because women produce more oxytocin, a biochemical that produces relaxation and nurturing. This suggests a gender differences in the activation of the sympatho-medullary pathway.

Typical mistake

Students, especially those with little knowledge of biology, often get the sympatho-medullary pathway (SMP) and pituitary adrenal system (PAS) confused. One helpful way of discriminating between them is to remember that the SMP is concerned with chronic or short-term stressors (e.g. a visit to the dentist) while the PAS is more concerned with chronic or long-term stressors, (e.g. constant financial worries).

Evaluation of the sympatho-medullary pathway

● A gender difference in the activation of the sympatho-medullary pathway may be due to women's evolutionary role in caring for children. If women fled or fought in response to stress, their children would be placed in danger, thus lowering reproductive success. A better response is to bond with other female group members for collective protection.

- Much SMP research is conducted on animals, which presents an extrapolation issue as humans are more likely to have a cognitive element to their stress responses. Also most human research has been conducted on males, as females' menstrual cycles involve hormonal fluctuations that produce stress responses which vary too widely to be considered valid. Such research is therefore non-generalisable to females.

The pituitary adrenal system

Revised ☐

Long-term chronic stressors activate the pituitary adrenal system (PAS), with the hypothalamus stimulating the production of corticotrophin-releasing hormone (CRH) into the bloodstream. This stimulates the pituitary gland to release adrenocorticotrophic hormone (ACTH), which travels to the adrenal glands, triggering the release of the stress hormone cortisol.

Cortisol elicits a steady supply of blood sugar to provide the body with a continuous source of energy to combat stressors and to tolerate elevated pain levels, though decreased cognitive and immune system functioning is also noticeable.

Newcomer et al. (1999) found that participants given cortisol in sufficient quantity to produce blood sugar levels similar to people undergoing major stress had a much reduced memory ability compared to participants given only sufficient cortisol to produce blood sugar levels that mimicked minor stress. This supports the idea that activation of the pituitary adrenal system incurs impaired cognitive functioning.

Watson et al. (2004) found that manic-depressives (people with bipolar disorder) had heightened cortisol levels, even in those where the condition was in remission, compared to non-sufferers. This suggests that dysfunction of the pituitary adrenal system may be involved in the disease process underlying the disorder.

Evaluation of the pituitary adrenal system

- Biological explanations of stress responses allow accurate, objective measures to be taken, such as those within the sympatho-medullary pathway and the pituitary adrenal system.
- It is difficult to generalise the results of research into stress responses as there are wide individual differences in responses. Mason (1975) found that different individuals produced different levels of stress hormones when subjected to exactly the same stressors.
- Chronic stressors that involve cognitive and emotional factors produce more active PAS responses. Symington et al. (1955) found that conscious terminal cancer patients experienced more stress than patients in a coma, which suggests that conscious patients have a more stressful cognitive appraisal of their condition.

Examiner's tip

Research studies can be used in two ways to comment upon bodily responses to stress. First, they can be used to outline *how* stress responses function (e.g. the sympatho-medullary pathway and the pituitary adrenal system). Second, they can be used to *evaluate* the responses (e.g. by explaining what conclusions can be drawn from such studies).

Stress-related illness

The immune system

Revised ☐

The **immune system** comprises of billions of cells produced in the spleen, lymph nodes, thymus and bone marrow travelling through the

immune system — bodily system that defends against disease

Exam practice answers and quick quizzes at **www.therevisionbutton.co.uk/myrevisionnotes**

blood stream to tissues and organs in order to protect the body against **antigens** (foreign bodies) like bacteria, cancerous cells and viruses.

Most immune system cells, in the presence of antigens, produce antibodies which bind to the antigens and destroy them. One such type of cell is the **leucocytes** (white blood cells).

Although cortisol itself protects against viruses and helps repair damaged tissues, prolonged stress causes over-production that weakens the immune system by reducing leucocyte activity and therefore the production of **antibodies (immunosuppression)**. Stress does not therefore actually cause illness, it simply reduces the immune system's ability to combat antigens. This leaves the body vulnerable to infectious illness such as influenza and chronic fatigue disorder.

Occasional production of cortisol and other corticosteroids does not harm the immune system.

Typical mistake

When unsure of the exact details, students often decline to write anything for fear of getting it wrong and being penalised. This is especially so in this area of psychology which asks for a lot of biological detail. However, examiners only use positive marking and award marks for what is correct. Errors and confusions will not *lose* marks. Better to write something and get a little credit than to write nothing and get no credit at all.

Kiecolt-Glaser (1984) took blood samples from students sitting stressful examinations and asked them to complete questionnaires. She found increased immunosuppression (measured by the amount of killer cell activity, a special type of leucocyte), especially in those scoring high on loneliness, stressful life events and psychiatric symptoms such as depression. This suggests that stress is linked to decreased immune system functioning, especially in individuals exposed to certain types of stressor.

Cohen et al. (1993) found that, of participants exposed to the cold virus, those with high stress scores were more likely to actually develop a cold. This implies that stress decreases the efficiency of the immune system, creating a greater vulnerability to illness.

Evans et al. (1994) found that short-term (acute) stress actually benefits the immune system, as students who gave mildly stressful public talks displayed increased levels of sigA, an antibody that enhances the ability of the immune system to resist infection.

Kiecolt-Glaser et al. (1995) found that slight wounds given to female participants who had the stress of caring for senile parents took longer to heal than those without such stressors. This finding was backed up by other measures of immune system functioning which suggests that prolonged chronic stress reduces immune system function.

Evaluation of stress and the immune system

- Most research linking stress to weakened immune system function is correlational and as such does not indicate causality. Other factors linked to an unhealthy lifestyle, such as smoking and drinking, may also play a part.

- Stress-related changes to immune system function may take time to develop and therefore might not be immediately identifiable by research. Longitudinal studies involving long-term measures of immune system function would be required to identify such changes.

- Findings gained from research into stress and the immune system can be used by health practitioners to predict problems relating to stress and to suggest appropriate coping strategies and therapies.

- Evidence does not indicate that all forms of stress damage the immune system. Although research does indeed show that chronic, long-term stress is strongly linked to immunosuppression and therefore heightened vulnerability to infection, the same is not necessarily true of acute, short-term stress. Indeed some research, such as Evans (1994), suggests that acute stressors can actually strengthen the immune system.

Typical mistake

When students answer examination questions referring to studies concerning the effects of stress on the immune system, they often concentrate on *how* the effects are created (i.e. the details of procedure). This is not advisable unless a question specifically asks for it. A more creditworthy approach is to summarise the main *findings and conclusions* of the studies.

Now test yourself

1 What type of stress do the sympatho-medullary pathway and the pituitary adrenal system deal with?
2 Outline in bullet point form how the SMP and the PAS work.
3 Why might there be a difference between how men and women react to stress?
4 Explain the role of the immune system and how it functions.
5 Explain how prolonged stress can damage the immune system and lead to illness.
6 Outline two pieces of research that suggest stress leads to immunosuppression (weakening of the immune system).

Answers on p. 105

Life changes and daily hassles

Most research into stress is conducted on stressors encountered in everyday life such as life changes (e.g. getting divorced) and daily hassles (e.g. commuting to work).

Life changes

The impact of **life changes** varies upon different individuals. For example the ending of a romantic relationship may be devastating for one person but a welcome release from constant trauma for another. Sometimes the fact that life changes do not occur is as stressful as when they do (e.g. failing to achieve a desired promotion at work).

Measuring scales that attempt to assess the effect of life changes objectively have been devised. The **social readjustment rating scale** (SRRS) was developed to investigate possible links between life changes and stress-related illnesses.

> **life changes** — occasional events incurring major adjustments to lifestyle

> **life change units** — measurement of amount of life-stress experienced in a given period

Holmes & Rahe (1967) examined the medical records of 5,000 patients, finding 43 common life changes which occurred prior to onset of illness. These life events were given ratings relating to how stressful they were perceived to be by 100 judges, the resulting scores being called **life change units** (LCUs) which made it possible to calculate the amount of stress an individual experiences in a given amount of time. Individuals with high LCU scores for the preceding 12 months had a heightened likelihood of experiencing illness in the following year. For example those with LCU scores of over 300 had an 80% chance of developing illnesses like diabetes, heart conditions and cancer. The research suggests that it is possible to measure stress objectively as an LCU score and that life changes are linked to stress-related illnesses.

Rahe et al. (1972) gave the social readjustment rating scale to 2,700 sailors to calculate the number of life changes experienced in the last 6 months. Medical records for the following 6-month tour of duty were then scrutinised, from which individual medical scores were compiled. A significant positive correlation between SRRS scores and medical scores was found, supporting the idea of a link between life changes and vulnerability to illness.

Li-Ping Tang & Hammontree (1992) assessed occupational stress levels and life changes in 60 police officers over a 6-month period, finding a positive correlation with absenteeism rates, which suggests a link between life stress and vulnerability to illness.

Evaluation of life changes as a source of stress

● Brown (1986) believes it might not be life changes themselves that are stressful, but unexpected, uncontrollable life changes. When people were asked to identify undesirable life changes from the social readjustment rating scale, only the ones identified as 'uncontrollable' correlated to developing later illness.

- Most research into life changes is correlational and does not indicate cause and effect relationships. An individual's general susceptibility to stress and their general health levels may also be important factors in determining vulnerability to illness.

- Most of the 43 life changes used to develop the SRRS are negative ones, especially those with high life change unit scores, so it may be that the SRRS confuses life changes with negativity.

- High LCU scores predict heightened risk of imminent illness, but not the nature of illness. Indeed different stress-related illnesses are associated with different types of stressor, which give a better indication of specific health risks.

- Many life change studies lack reliability, as they are dependent upon full and accurate memory, with participants having to recall past illnesses and stressful life events.

- Life events in the SRRS have set LCU scores, but individuals may experience life changes in different ways and to different degrees. The death of a loved one may be less traumatic and stressful if death releases that individual from constant pain.

Daily hassles

Revised

Stressful life changes are rare, with most stress coming from the irritations of **daily hassles** and as such are probably better indicators of health.

> **daily hassles** — everyday irritations that produce an overall heightened level of stress (e.g. traffic jams)

Daily hassles tend to accumulate, creating an overall elevated level of stress that incurs serious health risks. As well as hassles, daily life also has 'uplifts', positive occurrences, such as a good night's sleep, that can neutralise the negative effects of hassles.

Kanner et al. (1981) devised a hassles scale of 117 negative daily items and an uplifts scale of 135 positive items. One hundred participants were then studied over 12 months and it was found that daily hassles correlated with negative psychological symptoms and were a better indicator of illness than life changes. It was also found that life changes (e.g. divorce) led to daily hassles (e.g. having to cook, shop and clean for oneself) which then led to vulnerability to illness, suggesting that life changes and hassles interact to affect health levels.

De Longis et al. (1988) studied 75 married couples, finding no relationship between life changes and health, or between uplifts and health. However, hassles were associated with immediate health problems.

Sher (2004) found hassles were associated with heightened cortisol levels in healthy individuals and that increased cortisol contributed to the onset of depression in vulnerable individuals. This suggests that it is increased levels of stress hormones, due to hassles, which negatively affect health.

Van Houdenhove et al. (2002) found that chronic fatigue sufferers, compared to rheumatoid arthritis sufferers, were highly preoccupied and affected by daily hassles, which had a negative effect on self-image and interpersonal functioning. This suggests that hassles are related to specific conditions.

Examiner's tip

Research concerning the topic area of life changes and daily hassles mainly involves correlations and therefore does not show causality (cause and effect relationships), because such studies are not carried out under controlled conditions, meaning that other factors may be involved. Reference to this would be an effective means of detailing a weakness of research in this area, or as a form of evaluation in an essay question.

Evaluation of hassles

- The difference between daily hassles, like trying to find a seat on the train, and long-term stressors, like money problems, is difficult to see, but they may affect stress and health levels in very different ways.

- Research into hassles is dependent upon full and accurate memories. A solution is to ask participants to keep a diary and regularly record hassles and uplifts.

- Research tends to assess whether life changes or hassles have the biggest influence on health, when a better focus would be to concentrate on the effect they have on each other. For instance, someone experiencing a life change, like divorce, may find that daily hassles have a heightened stressful impact on well-being.

Workplace stressors

The workplace   Revised ☐

The workplace is a significant source of stress for many people, negatively impacting on health as well as decreasing productivity, whilst increasing absenteeism, accidents and staff-turnover. As well as directly affecting health and performance, **workplace stressors** also have an indirect effect by fostering unhealthy practices, such as heavy drinking. This has a financial cost to industry and the health services, as well as lowering the quality of an individual's life.

> **workplace stressors** — aspects of the work environment that have a negative life impact

Research has concentrated on identifying workplace stressors and their effect on health, in order that strategies can be put in place that lessen their impact. Important stressors identified include workload, predictability and controllability of work role, environmental factors and role conflict and ambiguity.

Johansson et al. (1978) found that Swedish sawmill workers whose jobs involved repetitiveness, high workload and high levels of responsibility, had high levels of stress hormones, stress-related illnesses and levels of absenteeism. This suggests that workplace stressors create long-term physiological arousal, leading to stress-related illnesses and absenteeism.

Marmot et al. (1997) used questionnaires and health screenings to find that civil servants with low job-control were three times more likely to have heart attacks than those with high job-control, implying that low job-control is harmful to health. However, Marmot found no correlation between workload and stress-related illness, which contradicts Johansson's (1978) findings. As Johansson focused on jobs that required continuous concentration, his findings may be a more valid measure of high workload.

Kivimaki et al. (2006) performed a meta-analysis involving 14 studies of 80,000 workers from America, Europe and Japan, finding that workers with high levels of job demand had a heightened risk of heart disease, further supporting the idea that workplace stressors increase vulnerability to illness.

Hobson & Beach (2000) asked managers at two factories to complete questionnaires and work diaries, finding that psychological health was not directly related to workload but was related to individual *perceptions* of workload. This suggests that it is *perceived* workload which better determines psychological health than actual workload, implying a cognitive element to workplace stressors.

Evaluation of workplace stressors

- The workplace in itself is not necessarily stressful and harmful to health. Indeed it can provide heightened opportunities for increased self-esteem, confidence and motivational levels and provide a sense of purpose and fulfillment that leads to psychological and physical well-being.

- Generally questionnaires are used to assess the effects of workplace stressors, but questionnaires place limits on the stressors respondents can comment on; interviews are superior as they permit a wider scope to report on individual experiences. Indeed interviews have identified other important stressors, like interpersonal clashes.

- Different individuals often experience the same stressors in different ways and to varying degrees, which may be related to an individual's perceived ability to cope with stressors, with 'hardy' personalities more able to cope (see *personality factors* below). This suggests there are individual differences in experiencing workplace stressors that research has failed to acknowledge.

- Research findings are quickly redundant due to the ever-changing nature of the workplace (e.g. increased technology, lower job security and altered work practices). Research therefore needs to be ongoing if it is truly to reflect the impact of workplace stressors.

Now test yourself

Tested ☐

7 What are life changes?

8 The social readjustment rating scale (SRRS) measures links between life events and stress-related illness in life change units (LCUs). Explain how LCUs were devised.

9 What research evidence is there that life changes can result in stress-related illness?

10 What is the difference between life changes and daily hassles?

11 Why might daily hassles be a better indicator of health than life changes?

12 Give details of two research studies into daily hassles and health.

13 What is meant by workplace stressors? Explain how they may affect health and performance at work.

14 Describe what research has found about the effects of workload and control.

Answers on p. 105

Personality factors

Personality consists of the characteristics that give individuals their unique identity and make them different from other individuals. Research indicates that individual differences in the way people perceive and respond to stressors are due in some part to differences in personality, differences broadly described in terms of **personality types**.

> **personality types** — broad characterisations describing categories of people sharing similar traits

Type A and Type B personalities

Revised ☐

Friedman and Rosenman (1959), in researching the role of non-biological factors in coronary heart disease, especially the role of individual differences in how men deal with stress (women having been found to be less vulnerable), discovered that a certain cluster of personality traits (see Table 4.1) was associated with heightened risk of contracting heart disease. This was referred to as **Type A personality**. Other minor Type A traits include: insecurity concerning status and a need to be admired by their peers in order to have good self-esteem.

> **Type A personality** — personality type characterised by time urgency, excessive competitiveness and generalised hostility, increasing risk of heart disease

Table 4.1 Main characteristics of Type A behaviour

Characteristic	Description
Time urgent	• Does several things at once • Constantly sets deadlines • Low boredom threshold
Excessive competitiveness	• Achievement orientated • Aggressive
General hostility	• Easily irritated • Volatile • Displays self-anger

From the same research the investigators identified **Type B personality**, which was the opposite of Type A personality in having the same degree of ambition, but in a steady non-competitive manner and being self-confident, relaxed, not driven to achieve perfection and being less hostile.

> **Type B personality** — healthy personality type characterised by non-competitiveness, self-confidence and relaxation
>
> **cardio-vascular disorders** — disorders of the heart and blood vessels

Examiner's tip

A common question on personality types would involve candidates having to tick boxes that link certain characteristics to certain personality types. You can prepare for these sorts of questions by making your own table of personality types and filling in the descriptive characteristics, or make a list of characteristics and learn which personality types they go with.

Friedman & Rosenman (1974) measured the personalities of over 3,500 healthy middle-aged males over a 12-year period, with those scoring highly on impatience, competitiveness, motivation for success, frustration at goals being blocked and aggressiveness under pressure, being labelled as Type A personality and low-scorers as Type B personality. Twice as many Type A personalities developed **cardiovascular disorders**, suggesting that personality is a risk factor in developing stress-related illness and that psychological factors exert a biological effect on the body, as the negative biological effects of stressors are mediated through psychological personality factors. Thus stressors are not harmful themselves, it is how individuals perceive and react to them that negatively affects health.

Hayes (2000) found that certain Type A characteristics correlated with specific types of cardio-vascular disorders. Angina sufferers had Type A characteristics of impatience and feeling pressurised at work, while heart-failure patients were hasty in their personal habits and schedules. This implies that particular Type A traits, rather than the personality type itself, are associated with specific heart conditions.

Matthews & Haynes (1986) found that coronary heart disease was most associated with the hostility trait of Type A men, especially those who do not reveal high levels of hostility. This supports Hayes' idea of particular Type A traits being associated with particular disorders. Further support comes from Forshaw (2002) finding the Type A trait of hostility to be the best single predictor of coronary heart disease and a better predictor than Type A personality as a whole.

Evaluation of Type A and Type B personality

- Some researchers could not replicate Friedman and Rosenman's results, but Miller et al. (1996) reviewed several studies and confirmed the original results.

- Although Type A men are more at risk of developing coronary heart disease, the risk is small and most will not develop the condition; Type B individuals are not immune to contracting it although at a lesser rate than Type A individuals.

- The idea of personality 'types' is an over-generalisation. It is more constructive to think in terms of specific personality traits as being stress-related risk factors.

- Friedman and Rosenman did not control for all aspects of lifestyle, so other factors like 'hardiness' (see below) may affect vulnerability to heart disease.

Typical mistake

It is quite easy, as many students do, to become confused by the terms 'personality' and 'behaviour' when referring to personality types and see them as separate things. Although some textbooks will refer for example to 'Type A personality' and other books to 'Type A behaviour' (and some even to both) they are actually the same thing. It is probably best to decide which term you are going to use and stick to it.

Exam practice answers and quick quizzes at **www.therevisionbutton.co.uk/myrevisionnotes**

- By 1988 Ragland and Brand found that 15% of Friedman and Rosenman's sample had died of coronary heart disease, with age, high blood pressure and smoking being important factors. However, they found little evidence that the Type A personality itself was related to the condition, weakening the idea of Type A personality being linked to stress-related illness.

Hardiness and other personality types

Revised

Kobasa (1979) proposed that people who experience high degrees of stress without becoming ill have a personality structure different from those who do become ill when stressed. Kobasa called this personality structure **hardiness**.

The 'hardy' personality type is characterised as having control over one's life, being committed to what one is doing and regarding stressors as enjoyable challenges that lead to self-improvement. Having a hardy personality type results in lowered physiological arousal in the presence of stressors and thus a reduction in stress-related disorders (see *stress management* page 66).

Type C personality is mainly associated with females and is characterised as conventional, pleasant, caring, helpful to others and who often repress their emotions when stressed. Research has associated this type with heightened vulnerability to cancer. **Type D personality** is referred to as a 'distressed' personality and is characterised by worry, irritability, gloom, lack of sociability and a tendency to negative emotions that are revealed to others, due to a fear of rejection and disapproval. Research has associated this type with heightened vulnerability to heart attacks.

> **hardiness** — healthy personality type characterised by control, commitment and self-improvement
>
> **Type C personality** — personality type characterised by suppression of negative emotions
>
> **Type D personality** — personality type characterised by distress, gloom, worry and lack of sociability

Kobasa (1979) found that highly stressed executives with low levels of illness had higher levels of hardiness than highly stressed executives with high levels of illness. This suggests that hardiness helps to protect against stress-related illness, a notion supported by Dreher (1995) finding that hardiness reduced illness by enhancing immune system function, which implies hardiness has a mediating effect upon stress.

Maddi et al. (1998) found that following hardiness training managers had increased hardiness and job satisfaction, while simultaneously displaying a decrease in severity of illnesses. Hardiness training also proved to be more effective than relaxation strategies and meditation, which suggests it is highly effective and can be learned.

Greer & Morris (1975) found that women with breast cancer suppressed their emotions more than women with non-fatal breast disorders, due to emotional suppression that led to a reduction in the efficiency of the immune system to resist disease. This was supported by Morris et al. (1981) finding that Type C women had an increased risk of developing cancer, which suggests that it is not just men who are prone to personality-related stress disorders. Further support came from Temoshok (1987) finding Type C personalities to be cancer prone, having problems expressing positive emotions and suppressing or inhibiting negative emotions, and Weinman (1985) who found that Type C personality traits influenced the progression of tumours and survival times.

Denollet et al. (1996) found that 53% of cardiac patients displayed Type D personality characteristics, which suggests the personality type is linked to an increased vulnerability to heart attacks. This was supported by Denollet et al. (1998) finding that Type D personality was associated with a 400% increased risk of sudden cardiac death, which was independent of other known risk factors, like smoking.

Examiner's tip

It is important to remember that you may also be able to use material on hardiness to answer questions on psychological methods of stress management. Because hardiness is seen as a personality type that can be learned (though some people may also have a naturally hardy personality) it can be regarded not only as a personality type in itself but also as a legitimate means of stress management.

Evaluation of hardiness and other personality types

- As hardiness can be learned, it suggests that teaching the personality type to those in highly stressful jobs may be cost effective and practical: the training would more than pay for itself in decreased illness rates, absenteeism, etc.
- Hardiness training is especially beneficial to those promoted to managerial positions, as promotion is often achieved without any knowledge of the stresses involved in management.
- There is no real evidence that people divide easily into separate personality types; indeed many people will display the traits of several types.
- Studying Type C women with cancer may be unethical in that it is adding stress to those already seriously ill. However, a cost-benefit analysis would argue such research to be desirable as it may help to create effective strategies that protect Type C personalities from developing tumours.

Stress management

Biological methods   Revised ☐

Biological methods of **stress management** focus directly on stress response systems like hormones and the autonomic nervous system. The symptoms of stress are directly addressed.

Drugs

Drugs reach the brain via the bloodstream, affecting neurotransmitter levels that effect communication between neurons. Anti-anxiety drugs combat stress by slowing central nervous system activity, suppressing the physical symptoms of anxiety.

When drugs have reduced symptoms of stress, psychological stress management methods can be added for further positive effects.

Benzodiazepines

Benzodiazepines (BZs) increase the effect of the **neurotransmitter** GABA in suppressing neural activity by stimulating an increase of chloride ions into brain neurons, making it difficult for other neurotransmitters to stimulate them. This creates a feeling of calm.

BZs also dampen the excitatory effect of the neurotransmitter serotonin, adding to the calming effect. They are a popular treatment, with over 2 million Britons being prescribed them. However, due to possible side-effects, such as dependency, BZs are only recommended for short-term use.

> **stress management** — physiological and psychological methods of dealing with the negative effects of stress
>
> **benzodiazepines** — anti-anxiety drugs that dampen down nervous system activity, creating a sense of calm (e.g. Valium)
>
> **neurotransmitters** — chemicals facilitating communication between brain nerve cells

Havoundjian et al. (1986) found that stressing rats resulted in rapid increases in the amount of chloride ions in the benzodiazepine–GABA receptor complex in the cerebral cortical membranes, thereby demonstrating the mechanisms by which acute stress operates. It is this response that benzodiazepine drugs have a moderating effect upon.

Davidson (1993) found that 78% of patients with social-anxiety disorders improved with drug treatment, compared to only 20% given a placebo treatment. A 2-year follow up found more effective functioning in those treated with BZs, demonstrating them to be effective as a long-term treatment.

Evaluation of benzodiazepines

- They were introduced to counteract the addictiveness of barbiturates but proved to be addictive themselves even at low doses, with severe withdrawal symptoms when treatment stops. Treatment should therefore not exceed 4 weeks. However a sizeable minority of patients use them in the long term, incurring a resultant risk of addiction.
- Like most drugs they are easy to take, cost-effective and popular with patients due to the familiarity of taking pills in everyday life.

Beta-blockers

When a person is anxious, increased adrenaline production stimulates the **beta-adrenergic receptors** (small structures occurring on cells in various body parts like the heart, brain and blood vessels). This stimulation results in increased heart rate. **Beta-blockers** (BBs) act upon beta-adrenergic receptors to block the transmission of nerve impulses by 'sitting on' the receptors to prevent them from being stimulated by adrenaline. This results in a reduction of both heart rate and the physically damaging effects of anxiety.

> **beta-blockers** — anti-anxiety drugs that block the transmission of nerve impulses, to reduce heart rate and alleviate the physical effects of stress
>
> **meta-analysis** — a review of similar research studies

> **Lau et al. (1992)** conducted a **meta-analysis**, finding beta-blockers to be effective in reducing high blood pressure. They reduced risk of death in heart disease patients by 20%, demonstrating their desirability as a treatment of cardiac disorders.
>
> **Lindholm et al. (2005)** used data from 105,000 participants to find that beta-blockers reduced the risk of strokes and were effective against heart problems, but that other anti-hypertension drugs were more effective in reducing risk of strokes.

Evaluation of beta-blockers

- They work immediately, acting directly to reduce heart rate and blood pressure and are therefore an effective treatment of potentially fatal cases of stress-related hypertension.
- Unlike benzodiazepines, they are not addictive but they can incur serious side-effects like hallucinations and cold extremities.

> **Examiner's tip**
>
> The research methodology of meta-analysis is regarded as good practice as it makes findings much more reliable and representative (i.e. the findings of one 'rogue', unrepresentative study are not relied on). A good means of evaluation, if evaluation is called for, is to refer to this point in your answer.

Psychological methods
Revised

Psychological methods aim to identify and address underlying psychological causes of stress-related disorders, with the focus on how individuals manage their perception of stress. Psychological methods come from different psychological approaches, each method reflecting how different approaches perceive the causes of stress-related disorders.

Stress-inoculation therapy

Stress-inoculation therapy (SIT) perceives some individuals as 'catastrophising' stress — misperceiving stressors as more damaging than they actually are — and therefore aims to enable such individuals to become immune to stressors by exposing them to a mildly stressful 'dose' of them.

SIT is a cognitive-behavioural method of stress management. **Cognitive-behavioural therapy** (CBT) involves cognitive restructuring, that is changing the means by which individuals think about themselves and their lives. The cognitive component involves being able to recognise stress symptoms, while the behavioural component involves using taught skills to deal with the causes of stress.

> **stress-inoculation therapy** — a type of cognitive-behavioural therapy that cognitively restructures emotional and behavioural responses
>
> **cognitive-behavioural therapy** — a psychological means of stress management that replaces irrational, maladaptive thought processes with rational, adaptive ones

SIT is fundamentally aimed at reducing stress through changing conditions (thought processes). It has three phases (see Table 4.2).

Table 4.2 Phases of stress-inoculation therapy

Phases	Description
Assessment	Patient and therapist (i) reduce stressors to individual components (ii) consider how stressors are thought about and dealt with (iii) consider how successful these are, with a common response being negative self-statements that create a self-defeating internal dialogue
Stress reduction techniques	Patients are taught skills to deal with stress (i) self-instruction (where coping self-statements are practised) (ii) direct action (where escape routes are arranged and relaxation exercises learned to reduce arousal) (iii) cognitive coping (where positive coping statements are learned to counteract negative self-statements)
Application and follow through	Patients practise using stress-reduction techniques as role play, then as real-life exercises, with stressors becoming increasingly more threatening

Jay & Elliot (1990) found that parents of leukaemia patients preparing for treatments who were taught stress-inoculation therapy skills via a video showed less anxiety and better coping skills than parents taught child-focused interventions, suggesting SIT to be an effective treatment of acute short-term stressors.

Holroyd et al. (1977) found that stress-inoculation therapy patients displayed better relief of chronic tension headaches compared to patients receiving physiological treatments, suggesting SIT to be an effective treatment of chronic long-term stressors.

Holcomb (1986) found stress-inoculation therapy to be more effective than drugs in reducing symptoms of depression, anxiety and distress. A 3-year follow up study found SIT patients required fewer admissions for psychiatric problems, suggesting SIT to be an effective long-term treatment.

Evaluation of stress-inoculation therapy

- It is difficult to ascertain which component of stress-inoculation therapy (relaxation, cognitive reappraisal, practical life skills etc.) is the most important in reducing stress symptoms.

- SIT is not a simple option as it requires motivation and commitment over long periods, not always easy for those suffering from stress-related disorders.

- Combat-based stress is not, generally, effectively treated by SIT as there is a stigma in the military in admitting to stress disorders and SIT programmes tend to be delivered as academic lectures, not an appropriate format for soldiers.

- SIT inoculates against future as well as current stressors, as it is effective over long periods and across different stressful situations. Skills can be practised and applied to a multitude of stressful situations.

Now test yourself

Tested ☐

15 Explain what research has suggested about stress-related illness and Type A personality.
16 Describe the characteristics of Type C and Type D personalities and explain what health disorders they are each associated with.
17 What is 'hardy' personality?
18 What has research suggested about hardy personalities?
19 Explain how BZs and BBs work.
20 How effective are drug treatments in combating the symptoms of stress disorders?
21 Outline what is meant by SIT.
22 Describe the three phases of SIT.
23 Does research suggest SIT to be effective?

Answers on p. 106

Exam practice

1 Copy and complete the accompanying table, placing a letter 'P' next to the two statements that relate to the pituitary-adrenal system and a letter 'S' next to the two statements that relate to the sympatho-medullary pathway. One statement will be left over. [4]

Statement	Letter
A system that responds to acute stressors	
Prepares the body for 'flight or fight' response	
A system involving the hormone cortisol	
The system that defends against disease	
A system that responds to chronic stressors	

2 Morag has had severe financial problems for the last year, problems that have become increasingly worse and from which she can see no way out. She feels physically and mentally tired and does not sleep well.

   With reference to the above statement, outline the effects of stress on the immune system. [6]

3 Outline what research has suggested about the relationship between daily hassles and stress-related disorders. [6]

4 Lewis works in a factory. Recently he has been demonstrating signs of stress-related illness. His doctor feels that certain features of the workplace are contributing to Lewis's illness.

   Outline three factors of workplace stress that may be contributing to Lewis's stress-related illness. [2 + 2 + 2]

5 Explain how Type A personality can contribute to stress-related illness. [4]

6 Discuss how personality factors affect the ways people react differently to stress. [12]

7 (a) Outline one psychological and one biological method of stress management. [4 + 4]

   (b) Explain one limitation of each method of stress management outlined in part (a). [2 + 2]

Answers and quick quiz 4 online

Online

Examiner's summary

✔ The sympatho-medullary pathway involves the body's response to short-term (acute) stressors, while the pituitary adrenal system deals more with long-term (chronic) stressors. Research studies can be used to both outline and evaluate these systems.

✔ The immune system's ability to protect against infection is severely reduced by stress, resulting in possible illness.

✔ Major life changes and the accumulation of minor daily hassles can elevate stress levels and incur serious health risks. Make reference to the social readjustment rating scale and the Kanner et al. hassles scale when commenting upon this stress/health risk link.

✔ Workplace stressors, like workload and control, are major sources of stress which can have either a negative impact on health either directly or indirectly.

✔ Better prepared candidates will be aware of research indicating how personality types affect the way individuals are influenced by stress. Type A characteristics are associated with heart disease, while Type B and hardiness characteristics are perceived as more healthy.

✔ Biological methods of stress management (e.g. drug treatments) impact directly upon stress response systems but have side-effects, while psychological methods (e.g. stress inoculation therapy) focus more on the underlying causes of stress-related disorders. Evaluation can be achieved by comparing these methods in terms of their effectiveness.

5 Social psychology — social influence

Conformity (majority influence)

Conformity occurs when an individual's behaviour and/or beliefs are influenced by a larger group. There is a need for individuals to agree so that groups can form and operate efficiently; conformity can however be a negative force that detracts from independence and incurs negative consequences.

> **conformity (majority influence)** — yielding to group pressures

Types of conformity   Revised ☐

Kelman (1958) made reference to three types of conformity that vary in the extent to which they affect belief systems (see Table 5.1). These are (i) **compliance**, (ii) **identification** and (iii) **internalisation**.

> **compliance** — public, but not private, agreement with majority influence to gain approval

Table 5.1 Types of conformity

Type of conformity	Description
Compliance	• Altering behaviour and opinions to that of a group to gain acceptance/avoid rejection, for example wearing your local football team's replica shirt • Weak, temporary form of conformity that is only displayed in the presence of the group • Involves public, but not private, acceptance of the group's behaviour and attitudes
Identification	• Altering behaviour and opinions to that of a group, as group membership is desirable, for example to gain promotion at work • A stronger form of conformity involving public and private acceptance of the group's behaviour and attitudes • Temporary form of conformity that is not maintained outside the group, for example adopting the behaviour and beliefs of fellow soldiers when joining the army, but not after returning to civilian life
Internalisation	• Truly altering behaviour and opinions to that of a group, for example conversion to religious beliefs such as Buddhism • Involves acceptance of group's belief system • A strong form of conformity involving public and private acceptance of the group's behaviour and attitudes that is not dependent on the presence of the group for maintenance

Examiner's tip

A common question for this topic would be to ask candidates to tick boxes or enter information into boxes concerning types of conformity. You can therefore practise for this by constructing your own table and entering the relevant information.

> **identification** — public and private agreement with majority influence to gain acceptance
>
> **internalisation** — public and private agreement with majority influence due to adopting the majority's belief system

Explanations of conformity

Explanations of conformity are concerned with what motivates individuals to conform.

Normative social influence

Revised

The motive underlying **normative social influence** (NSI) is the desire to be accepted by others and to avoid rejection which, from an evolutionary point of view, has a survival value. NSI entails getting others to like and respect us and the best way to achieve this is to agree with others' views. NSI does not necessarily indicate true agreement (compliance) and can involve making a compromise between our own opinions and those of others (see Asch's study, page 72). It can therefore be seen as a fairly weak form of conformity.

> **normative social influence** — a motivational force to be liked and accepted by a group

Informational social influence

Revised

Humans have a need for certainty, to feel that their beliefs and behaviours are correct, as this allows them to feel they are in control of their environment which, from an evolutionary point of view, has a survival value. When in uncertain or new situations individuals look to others for guidance as how to think and behave (e.g. how to vote in your first election). **Informational social influence** (ISI) generally involves being 'converted' to the views of others (internalisation) and is therefore is a relatively stronger form of conformity (see Jenness's study page 72).

> **informational social influence** — a motivational force to look to others for guidance as to how to behave in uncertain situations

Cognitive dissonance

Revised

Cognitive dissonance is caused by simultaneously holding two contradictory ideas (cognitions). Altering cognitions so they become compatible with each other reduces cognitive dissonance; this can be achieved by conformity.

> **cognitive dissonance** — an unpleasant feeling of anxiety created by simultaneously holding two contradictory ideas

Individual differences

Revised

People with low self-esteem, need for approval and feelings of insecurity, high anxiety and self-blame are associated with high levels of conformity due to their need for group acceptance and low levels of independent thought. Several researchers have found that women conform more, possibly because females have an evolutionary higher drive for co-operation. However, some researchers believe this finding is due to flawed methodology where male researchers got participants to conform to male type activities that are unfamiliar to females who then conform due to ISI.

> **Typical mistake**
>
> Students generally have good knowledge of types of conformity and of research studies into conformity but do not know which studies relate to which specific type of conformity. Asch and Crutchfield are mainly studies of normative social influence; Jenness and Sherif are more applicable to informational social influence. Better candidates will explain that these studies have elements of both and would to refer to specific features of the studies to gain high-level credit.

Cultural factors

Research indicates that people from collectivist cultures and those from cultures characterised by high levels of co-operation are more conformist, as well as those from cultures with a high degree of similarity of beliefs and attitudes.

Asch (1955) investigated the extent to which individuals conform to an obviously wrong answer. One hundred and twenty-three male students were tested individually in groups of seven to nine confederates, the real participant answering last or second last. Participants had to select which of three stimulus lines matched a comparison line. On 12 out of 18 trials the confederates gave an identical incorrect answer. An overall conformity rate of 32% was found, with 75% of participants conforming at least once. 25% never conformed and 5% conformed on all 12 occasions. The findings suggest normative social influence occurs, involving public, but not private, acceptance of others' opinions (compliance) in order to avoid ridicule/rejection.

Jenness (1932) investigated how discussion with others would affect judgements in an ambiguous (uncertain) situation. Participants made individual estimates of jelly-beans in a jar and then discussed their judgements in groups to arrive at a group estimate, before making second individual estimates. Typicality of opinion was found where second individual estimates moved closer to the group estimate, with greater conformity among females. The findings suggest informational social influence occurs, involving public and private acceptance (internalisation) by looking to the opinions of others in order to be correct.

Bogdonoff et al. (1961), using an Asch-type procedure, assessed the amount of stress produced by measuring galvanic skin response (GSR), finding heightened stress levels in participants when faced with a majority opinion that seemed incorrect. However, stress levels decreased with conformity, which supports the idea that conformity can sometimes occur due to a reduction in cognitive dissonance by reducing the inconsistency between two incompatible cognitions (one's own beliefs and the beliefs of others).

Eagly & Carli (1981), like Jenness, found women to be more conformist, which suggests that men display more independent behaviour. However Eagly & Chrvala (1986) found that older women are more conformist than older men, but that younger women are no more conformist than younger men, which implies that factors other than gender, such as age, may be involved.

Berry (1967) found that the Temne people of Sierra Leone are more conformist than the Innuits of Canada, a fact he related to the nature of economic subsistence in the two cultures. The Temne rely on a single crop that requires high levels of co-operation to cultivate, while the Innuits hunt in an individualistic manner. This suggests that culturally determined degrees of co-operation contribute to conformity levels.

Evaluation of explanations of conformity

- Normative social influence, informational social influence and cognitive dissonance can explain most, if not all, real-life examples of conformity, lending support to them as explanations of conformity.

- Perceiving NSI, ISI and cognitive dissonance as separate and sole explanations of conformity is simplistic, as generally more than one explanation will be relevant. For instance in Asch's study (above) the conformity can be seen as informational and normative: participants looked to others for correct information and to gain their acceptance.

- Conformity can have negative effects, for example NSI can lead to inter-group violence, such as gang wars. However, it is only by understanding how and why such acts occur that practical applications can be created that stop such behaviour, or even prevent it occurring in the first place.

- NSI can explain how individuals develop positive and negative attitudes to different groups by their degree of social desirability and acceptability.

- Conformity due to reduction of cognitive dissonance can be seen as healthy, as it reduces stress levels.

Examiner's tip

If an examination question focuses upon *research studies*, like those relating to conformity or obedience, then it would be highly creditworthy to comment on methodological issues as part of your evaluation (e.g. ecological validity).

If, however, a question focuses upon *explanations*, like those of conformity or obedience, then it would be better to focus evaluation directly on their value as explanations (e.g. on the degree of research support).

Variations and replications of Asch's paradigm

Revised

Asch established the accepted method (paradigm) of studying conformity. He found that with one participant and one confederate, conformity was low, but with two confederates conformity rose to 13% and with three confederates to 32%. After that, adding more confederates did not increase conformity.

Gerard et al. (1968) disagreed, however, finding that increasing the number of participants did increase conformity, although the rate of conformity decreased with each additional confederate.

Asch found that if one confederate gave correct answers, conformity dropped to 5.5% and if one confederate disagreed with both the real participant and the other confederates, conformity declined to 9%, which suggests that it is the reduction of the majority's consensus (agreement) that is the important factor. He also found that making the task more difficult by giving similar comparison levels increased conformity, but this probably made it more a case of informational social influence than normative social influence.

Finally, Asch found that asking participants to write answers down rather than say them aloud reduced overall conformity to 12.5%, which suggests that ridicule and disapproval are important factors.

Larsen (1974) used the Asch paradigm on American students, getting a considerably lower conformity rate; and yet when repeating the study in 1979 he found a similar conformity rate to Asch. This suggests that social changes over time affect conformity rates.

Perrin & Spencer (1981) found only a 0.25% conformity rate using the Asch paradigm on British science students. This may be because science students are taught to question things. When the researchers repeated the study on institutionalised young offenders, a group who lacked independent thought, a conformity rate similar to Asch's was found.

Bond & Smith (1996) performed a meta-analysis of 134 Asch replications from 17 countries to compare conformity rates across different cultures. They also compared 97 replications performed in the USA at different times. A steady decline in conformity over time was found within the USA and independent cultures showed lower conformity rates than collectivist ones. This suggests that conformity reflects the degree of independence within a culture and that conformity rates reflect social change within a given culture over time.

Evaluation of conformity studies

- Asch's paradigm is uneconomical as it only tests one participant at a time. Crutchfield (1954) conducted similar research, but with a procedure that tested several participants simultaneously.

- Asch's paradigm is unrealistic and thus lacks ecological validity (see page 47). It would be unlikely that such a task would ever occur in everyday life.

- Asch's paradigm is unethical as it involves deceit. Participants thought the confederates were fellow participants and that it was a study of visual perception. The study also created stress within participants when faced with a conflicting majority influence.

- Asch's findings are unrepresentative as the study only involved American male students. Research suggests conformity rates change across cultures and that females conform more. The study is also a product of its time (the 1950s) as research suggests that conformity alters with social change.

Typical mistake

Many students refer to Asch's study as an 'experiment' but it is not. It has no independent variable and is therefore more of a controlled observation. However, it can be regarded as an experiment if Asch's variations are considered, with the independent variable being the particular variation performed and the dependent variable being the degree of conformity. Reference to this would make excellent evaluation of Asch.

- As the overall conformity rate in Asch's study was only 32%, the majority of people are independent rather than conformist. Indeed 25% of participants never conformed.

- Unlike most studies of social influence, Jenness's study is ethical as it does not involve an element of deceit. However the study tells us little about conformity in situations where there is an obviously correct answer. For that we need to look to Asch.

- Jenness's main finding (that people look to others in uncertain situations) is backed up by Sherif (1935) who found that when participants were asked to estimate how much a dot of light in a dark room moved (it did not move at all), their individual estimates moved closer together after hearing each others' first estimates.

- Several researchers have found that women conform more. However it may be that women are more socially oriented to agree and co-operate than men or that females are less certain of their judgements in ambiguous situations. The finding may also be a product of methodology as most studies involve face-to-face situations that do not often occur in real-life or experimental situations created by male researchers that are unfamiliar to female participants, creating informational social influence in female participants but not in male ones.

Now test yourself

Tested

1 Why does compliance occur?
2 What type of conformity involves (i) individuals truly converting to the belief system of others? (ii) public, but not private, acceptance of a group's behaviour and attitudes?
3 What type of conformity (i) is maintained without the presence or influence of the majority influence? (ii) occurs because membership of the group is desirable?
4 Why is identification a stronger form of conformity than compliance, but a weaker form than internalisation?
5 How does NSI differ from ISI as an explanation of conformity?
6 What is cognitive dissonance and how can it be used as an explanation of conformity?
7 Outline other explanations of conformity.

Answers on p. 106

Obedience

Obedience can be a good thing; indeed society cannot function in a meaningful way without (i) rules and laws that people follow and (ii) general recognition of which people hold legitimate authority and have the right to give orders. Obedience can, however, be a negative force for destruction. After the Second World War, psychologists turned their attention to understanding the holocaust, where Germans unquestioningly followed the orders of the Nazis to exterminate millions of Jews, Gypsies and other people seen as *untermenschen* (sub-human).

> **obedience** — complying with the demands of an authority figure, changing behaviour in response to another person's direct instructions

Milgram's research into obedience

Revised

Milgram, a student of Asch, was a Jewish working-class New Yorker, whose family escaped the Nazi holocaust. He was motivated to understand whether it was a German personality defect that had led to blind obedience to commit genocide, or that people generally could be manipulated to obey destructive orders they did not necessarily agree with.

Milgram (1963)

Procedure: a volunteer sample of 40 males aged 20–50 years was obtained to take part in a supposed study of memory and learning at Yale University. Participants were tested individually, with a rigged draw ensuring that the participant was always the 'teacher' and a confederate (fake) participant the 'learner'. A confederate 'experimenter' wearing a laboratory coat was seemingly in charge.

The learner was strapped into a chair in an adjoining room and the teacher instructed to give an electric 'shock' to the learner each time a question was answered incorrectly. The 'shocks' were actually fake but the teacher was given a real 45-volt shock to convince him they were real. The learner was initially agreeable and the fake shocks went up in 15-volt increments from 0 to 450 volts. Any time the teacher considered not continuing the experimenter used verbal prods, such as 'you have no choice, you must go on', to command the teacher to carry on. At 300 volts the learner claimed to have heart problems and refused to answer questions. After 315 volts he screamed loudly and after 330 volts was heard from no more.

Quantitative findings: 100% of participants went up to 300 volts and 62.5% went up to the maximum 450 volts (which was given 4 times). *Qualitative findings:* Many participants ('teachers') showed distress and argued with the 'experimenter'. Three had seizures.

Conclusions: (1) The 'Germans are different' hypothesis is false. (2) Obeying orders from a perceived legitimate authority is normal behaviour. (3) People will obey orders that they morally disagree with.

Milgram (1974) carried out a series of variations to identify the important variables, which showed that situational factors affect obedience rates (see Table 5.2).

Table 5.2 Milgram's variations

Variation	% Obeying	Comments
Standard procedure	62.5%	The standard procedure
Learner is silent throughout	100%	Highest rate of obedience seen
Study occurs in run-down office block	48%	The prestigious setting of Yale University gives a sense of legitimate authority
Learner in same room as teacher	40%	Increasing proximity decreases obedience
Teacher forces learner's hand onto shock-plate	30%	More increased proximity again decreases obedience
Experimenter not present, but phones orders in	20.5%	Proximity to authority figure is important
Two other confederate teachers present who refuse to obey	10%	Disobedient models have a large influence
Teacher reads out the questions, a confederate teacher gives the shocks	92.5%	Obedience is high when responsibility for actions is seemingly held by another

Evaluation of Milgram

- Milgram (like Asch for conformity) established the **Milgram paradigm** (accepted method) for studying obedience. Milgram's paradigm has been used in many countries. Although differences in methodology make comparisons difficult, varying rates of obedience were found (e.g. as high as 90% in Spain, but as low as 40% in Australia). This suggests a reflection of cultural differences in attitudes towards authority.

- Milgram's original study was intended as a pilot study, but he didn't expect such astounding results (pre-study estimates by experts were of around 1% obedience). Therefore his variations, which were stimulated by the original findings, can be regarded as the 'proper' study. Milgram hoped his findings would lead to strategies to resist blind obedience. Alas, not much has changed. Countless people die every day as a result of 'unthinking obedience'.

> **Milgram paradigm** — experimental procedure devised by Stanley Milgram for measuring obedience rates

There are several criticisms of Milgram's methodology.

1 Orne and Holland (1968) criticised the internal validity of the study as they believed participants only gave the shocks knowing them to be false. However the fact that only 20% of participants expressed any doubts, the intense reactions of participant 'teachers' (remember three had seizures), the real 45-volt shock given to participants and the apparent authenticity of the shock generator all suggest they believed the shock to be real.

2 The study can be said to lack mundane realism, as it is not an everyday occurence to be asked to give electric shocks to people. Hofling (1966), however, conducted a real-life study by asking 22 nurses if they would break hospital rules and give an overdose of a drug if ordered to by a doctor; 21 said no. Then 22 other nurses were phoned individually by a supposed doctor and ordered to give an overdose of an unfamiliar drug without signed authorisation (the drug was actually harmless); 21 obeyed, which suggests that people do obey authority figures in real-life situations. However, Rank and Jacobsen (1977) repeated the study with a familiar drug, allowing the nurses to consult each other. Only 2 out of 18 nurses obeyed in this situation, which suggests that Hofling's study did not have external validity after all.

3 The findings only relate to American culture; replications in other cultures have found widely differing obedience rates.

4 The findings only relate to males, as only male participants were used; indeed replications involving females have often found even higher obedience rate.

> **Typical mistake**
>
> As with Asch's study, many students refer to Milgram's original study as an experiment but it is not as it has no independent variable. It should be referred to as a controlled observation. However, it can be perceived as an experiment if Milgram's variations are considered, with the independent variable being the variation performed and the dependent variable being the obedience rate.

There are several ethical criticisms of Milgram's study:

1 **Harm** — Milgram was accused of subjecting participants to severe stress and harm. However, only 2% expressed regrets at being involved and 74% thought they learned something useful. A full debriefing took place and a psychiatric assessment one year later found no long-term damage.

2 **Deception and lack of informed consent** — participants were deceived about the purpose of the study, the confederates, the assignment of roles and the fake shocks. Therefore informed consent could not be gained. Milgram defended the deception as necessary for the study to have value and carried out a full debriefing.

Exam practice answers and quick quizzes at **www.therevisionbutton.co.uk/myrevisionnotes**

3 **Right to withdraw** — Milgram said there was a right to withdraw, as 37.5% of participants refused to carry on. However, no right to withdraw was mentioned and verbal prods were used to discourage participants from doing so.

Milgram had his membership of the American Psychological Association suspended, though the study was later classed as ethically acceptable and he won a top award. Perhaps what critics objected to was not the lack of ethics but the uncomfortable results that went against the idea of free will.

Explanations of why people obey

- **Situational factors** — Milgram's studies show that reasons for obedience lie in aspects of the situation, rather than the personality of a person. For example in Milgram's study obedience was high at the prestigious Yale University, but low in a less prestigious run-down office block.

- **Perception of legitimate authority** — people tend to obey authority figures who possess symbols of power and status, such as the laboratory coat of Milgram's 'experimenter' or a high-ranking army officer.

- The **agentic state** — when obeying, people see themselves as agents of the authority figure's wishes. The agentic state is when they give up personal responsibility of the **autonomous state** and transfer responsibility to the authority figure. 'I was only following orders' was the defence given by Nazi war criminal Albert Eichmann for his organisation of the holocaust.

> **agentic state** — acting as an agent of another who is therefore seen as responsible for the behaviour
>
> **autonomous state** — opposite of the agentic state, where individuals see themselves as responsible for their actions

- **Personal responsibility** — when people are made to feel more personally responsible for their actions (part of the autonomous state), obedience will decline. In Milgram's study obedience declined when the learner was in the same room, even more so when his hand was forced onto a shock plate. However, obedience was high when the teacher only read out the questions and someone else gave the shocks.

- **Gradual commitment** — the more people comply with apparently small acts of obedience, the harder it becomes to refuse further orders with more severe consequences. After giving seemingly mild shocks of 15, 30, 45-volt etc shocks it becomes increasingly harder to refuse to give more severe shocks.

- **Dehumanisation** — it is easier to obey orders to harm those seen as lesser people. The Nazis characterised the Jews and Gypsies as 'sub-human' so that it was easier to comply with orders to kill them. Some participants in Milgram's study commented 'he was so stupid he deserved to be shocked'.

> **Examiner's tip**
>
> You need to understand what the 'command' words in questions mean in order to answer correctly. For instance *identify* means merely 'to name', *define* means 'what is meant by', *outline* means 'give brief details without explanation', *describe* means 'give a detailed account without explanation', *analyse* means 'examine in detail', while *evaluate* means 'assess the value or effectiveness of'.

Now test yourself

8 Explain how obedience can be (i) a force for good (ii) a negative force for destruction.
9 Outline the aims, procedure, findings and conclusions of Milgram's study.
10 Outline the findings of Milgram's variations.
11 Outline explanations of obedience, giving an example of each from Milgram's study.

Answers on p. 107

Explanations of independent behaviour

Independent behaviour refers to (1) **resistance to conformity** (non-conformity) and (2) **resisting obedience** (showing disobedience to authority figures).

Resisting conformity

Non-conformity can either involve (i) **independence** — movement neither towards or away from social expectancy (i.e. doing your own thing and not being influenced by others) or (ii) **anti-conformity** — movement away from social expectancy (i.e. adopting the behaviours and norms of a minority group); this is actually conformist, in that there is dependence on a minority group's norms in opposition to a majority group's norms.

Dissent

Dissent is a form of resistance that involves the presence of an individual or individuals who publicly disagree with and go against the majority. In situations where an individual finds themselves subjected to pressures to conform to majority influence, it is easier to resist such pressures if there is a dissenting other or others.

> **Examiner's tip**
>
> Generally any factors that can be seen as reducing conformity or obedience can also be seen as ways of resisting conformity and obedience, for example the presence of dissenting confederates in social influence research studies. As long as such material is specifically shaped to the requirements of a question involving resistance, it will gain credit.

In one of **Asch's variations** to his 1955 study (see page 72) the presence of a dissenting confederate caused conformity rates to drop sharply (from 32% down to 5.5% overall conformity on the critical trials), even if they also did not agree with the real participant (down to 9% overall conformity on the critical trials). It therefore seemed to be the act of dissenting that freed up participants to give their true answers. This suggests that a major way of resisting conformity is to break up the unanimous agreement of the majority.

Allen & Levine (1971) found conformity rates decreased on a task involving visual judgements, even if the dissenter wore glasses with thick lenses and confessed to having problems with vision, which indicates that conformity is reduced even if dissenters do not appear particularly skilled or competent. This again suggests it is the act of dissenting that is important, as it gives moral support to other people to dissent from the majority opinion.

Baron & Byrne (1991) found that earlier support received from dissenters is more effective in resisting conformity than support received later. This suggests that in situations where pressures to conform increase, it is easier to resist such majority influence sooner rather than later on. Earlier dissent seems to have more of a rallying effect in getting others to resist. This is similar to the phenomenon of gradual commitment, where people who comply with initial orders of obedience find it increasingly harder to resist subsequent orders of obedience which have more severe consequences and may violate people's personal moral codes.

Other factors in resisting conformity

1 **Reactance** — when people's freedom of choice is restricted they often respond with **reactance**. Hamilton et al. (2005) found that adolescents who were told it was okay to smoke if they were aware of the health risks were less likely to smoke than those told never to smoke.

2 **Ironic deviance** — if people believe the source of informational influence is not genuine, then they will resist such influence — **ironic deviance**. Conway and Shaller (2005) found that office workers would use a software product if others recommended it, but not if they believed they were recommending it after being ordered to by their manager.

3 **Status** — individuals of higher status within a group are more likely to resist majority influence. Low-status members, such as newcomers to a group, are motivated to achieve higher status by conformist behaviour.

> **reactance** — rebellious anger produced by attempts to restrict freedom of choice
>
> **ironic deviance** — the belief that if other people behave in certain ways because they have been told to do so, it reduces their informational influence

Richardson (2009) found that low-status newcomers to a group were more likely to conform to an obviously poor recommendation if it was made by apparently high-status confederates than low-status ones.

Resisting obedience

Revised

1. **Decreasing agentic state** — anything that detracts from an authority figure's perceived legitimate authority decreases the agentic state and increases the autonomous state, making obedience less likely. For example in Milgram's variations when the experimenter was not present but gave orders by phone, obedience rates declined.

2. **Increasing personal responsibility** — anything that makes an individual feel more accountable for their actions also decreases the agentic state and increases the autonomous state, making obedience less likely. For example when Milgram's participants could see the effects of their shocks, obedience rates declined.

3. **Modelling** — resistance to obedience can also occur through modelling, where behaviour in others is observed and imitated. In Milgram's variations when two confederate teachers refused to obey, they acted as models of disobedience, demonstrating that it was possible to do so and how to do it.

4. **Systematic processing** — individuals are less likely to obey if they can consider what they have been ordered to do. Marin et al. (2007) found that if participants were encouraged and permitted to consider the content of unreasonable orders, then they were less likely to comply.

5. **Morality** — individuals whose behaviour is based on moral principles are more resistant to destructive obedience. Kohlberg (1969) gave moral dilemmas to participants in the Milgram study, finding those who based decisions on personal moral codes were less obedient.

6. **Experience** — individuals who have experience of the consequences of destructive obedience are more likely to disobey. An electrician in Milgram's study refused to comply, as he was aware of what such voltages could do to a person, while another participant disobeyed, as she'd lived through the Nazi regime and had first hand experience of the consequences of such blind obedience.

7. **Personality** — some personality traits are more associated with resisting obedience. Milgram (1974) proposed the authoritarian personality, characterised as prejudiced against minorities, rigid, inflexible and submissive to higher-status individuals. Those with opposite traits are therefore more resistant to obedience.

> **Examiner's tip**
>
> Questions that ask for explanations/strengths/weaknesses/factors generally tend to be worth 3 marks. To ensure that you earn all the marks available, you need to elaborate your answer. This entails making a valid point (e.g. identifying a factor involved in resisting conformity) then explaining it to show understanding and finally providing research evidence (or a real life example) that illuminates the point further.

Locus of control

Revised

Locus of control (LOC) was proposed as a personality dimension by Rotter (1966) and concerns the degree to which people perceive themselves as in charge of their lives.

Individuals with high **internal LOC** believe they personally can affect the outcomes of situations, while those with high **external LOC**

> **locus of control** — an individual's beliefs about the causes of successes and failures

believe they have no influence over circumstances. Internal LOC refers to the extent to which people think outcomes are based on their own efforts, choices and decisions, while external LOC concerns the degree to which individuals see outcomes as resulting from fate, luck and other uncontrollable influences.

Rotter (1966) saw those possessing a high internal LOC as being more resistant to social influence because such individuals perceive themselves as in control of situations and therefore believe they have freedom of choice over whether to conform and obey.

> **Typical mistake**
>
> When writing about locus of control it is easy to fall into the trap of merely outlining the material without explicitly linking it to independent behaviour. Always read through your answers to ensure they really are answering the question.

Shute (1975) exposed undergraduate students to peers expressing negative or positive views to drug-taking, finding that participants with an internal locus of control were more able to resist conforming to peers with pro-drug attitudes. This supports the view that having high internal LOC increases resistance to conformity.

Moghaddam (1998) found that the Japanese conform more than Americans and have higher levels of external locus of control, which suggests that cultural differences in conformity rates may be attributable to differences in LOC.

Jones & Kavanagh (1996) found that individuals with low external locus of control were more able to resist obeying immoral authority figures. This suggests an explanation for corporate fraud, where lower-status workers with high external locus of control are more susceptible to obeying orders to perform illegal actions.

Avtgis (1998) conducted a meta-analysis of locus of control and conformity studies, finding that those with high external LOC were more persuadable and prone to conformity, which implies that differences in LOC are related to differences in levels of conformist behaviour.

Twenge et al. (2004) reported that Americans have developed higher levels of external locus of control due to higher incidences of suicide, divorce and mental illness. This implies that Americans are becoming less independent in their behaviour and thus less resistant to conformity and obedience.

Understanding social change

Social change occurs when society embraces new behaviours and beliefs and is a gradual, ongoing process as minority viewpoints increase and eventually become the majority opinion. Social change can either be positive (e.g. the Suffragette movement gaining votes for women), or negative (e.g. the acceptance of illegal interrogation methods by the military at Abu Ghraib prison in Iraq).

> **social change** — the processes by which society changes beliefs, attitudes and behaviour to create new social norms (expected modes of thought and behaviour)

How social change can occur   Revised

There are several ways in which social influence research suggests that social change can occur.

The promotion of group status

Promoting group status is a method of achieving positive social change. Tajfel (1981) introduced the concept of **social identity theory**, which divided social groups into in (**us**) and out (**them**) groups. A group can change a negative image held by outsiders to a positive one by promoting social change. For example people outside their social grouping initially had a negative perception of West Indian immigrants to Britain in the 1950s. However, by contributing positively to society and promoting their worth to the community (e.g. providing successful sporting and musical role models) West Indians developed a more positive image within mainstream British society.

Exam practice answers and quick quizzes at **www.therevisionbutton.co.uk/myrevisionnotes**

Rebellious role models

The use of rebellious role models (e.g. dissenting confederate teachers in Milgram's variations and dissenting confederate participants in Asch's variations) demonstrates how obedience and conformity levels can be lowered, decreasing the level of negative social change which occurs.

Reversal of gradual commitment

Zimbardo (2007) proposed reversal of gradual commitment (see p. 77) as a means of promoting positive social change. Milgram (1963) demonstrated how gradual commitment steadily drew participants into becoming increasingly obedient to instructions to perform actions with negative consequences.

Zimbardo proposed that individuals could equally be encouraged to indulge in positive actions by a reversal of this process, like gradually encouraging people in a step-by-step process to involve themselves in recycling household rubbish.

Exposure to models of independent behaviour

Nemeth and Chiles (1988) proposed that by exposing individuals to models of independent behaviour they are taught to become more independent and thus more resistant to attempts to promote conformity and obedience levels which could incur negative social change.

The role of minority influence

How minority influence works
Revised ☐

Minorities incur social change by altering attitudes and behaviour over time, creating long-lasting forms of conformity that involve fundamental changes in belief systems. In this way **innovation** occurs, with new ideas and behaviours becoming adopted as mainstream practices, with the process requiring minorities to be *consistent*, *flexible*, *committed* and *relevant*.

The gradual process by which minority opinions become majority ones is known as **social cryptoamnesia** (the snowball effect). Initially, converts to the minority viewpoint are few and slow to occur, but as more individuals change their attitude to that of the minority group, the pace picks up, with the minority gaining status, influence, power and acceptability. For example, the environmental group Greenpeace was formed in Canada in the 1970s and was originally mocked as a bunch of cranks. However over time the group increasingly gained members and popular support until eventually it was universally perceived as the legitimate viewpoint on environmental issues.

> **minority influence** — a type of social influence that motivates individuals to reject established majority group norms

Moscovici et al. (1969) investigated the role of minority group influence on the process of innovation by testing 32 groups of 6 female participants, of whom 2 in each group were confederates. Each group was shown 36 blue slides of different intensities, with participants stating the colours of the slides out aloud and in front of the rest of the group.

- Condition one — the 2 confederates consistently claimed all the slides were green
- Condition two — the 2 confederates were inconsistent, claiming 12 slides were blue and 24 were green
- Condition three — the 2 confederates claimed all the slides were green, but the real participants gave their answers privately
- Results — In condition one 8.42% of participants agreed with the minority, with 32% agreeing on at least one occasion, while in condition two only 1.2% of participants agreed with the minority. Interestingly in condition three there was greater private agreement with the minority than in public.
- Conclusions — minority groups can influence majority opinion, especially if the minority is consistent in its opinions. Consistent minorities have most influence over private attitudes and opinions.

Meyers et al. (2000) supported Moscovici by finding that minority groups that were most successful in influencing majority opinion were consistent in their views.

Martin et al. (2003) found that messages with minority group support were more resistant to change than if supported by a majority group. This implies that cognitive processing of minority opinions leads to the formation of attitudes that are resistant to counter-persuasion, demonstrating the power of minorities to incur social change.

Martin & Hewstone (1996) reported that minority influence led to more creative and novel judgements than majority influence, supporting the idea that minority influence is a force for innovation and social change.

Kruglanski (2003) believes terrorism is a form of minority influence incurring social change, with terrorist organisations using several factors of minority group persuasion to promote their ideals, being consistent and persistent in their actions, achieving internalisation of their beliefs as legitimate ones and using the zeitgeist (spirit of the times) to take advantage of a common groundswell of support. For example the IRA was portrayed by the British government as a small group of violent extremists, when in reality their campaign of bombings and assassinations had considerable support among nationalist communities in Northern Ireland, demonstrated by the steady growth in electoral support for Sinn Fein, the political wing of the IRA.

Evaluation

- Minorities are influential, as they often have deeply held convictions, have made sacrifices in holding their viewpoints and may be perceived as highly principled, causing the majority to think about issues they otherwise might not.

- Moscovici's findings may not be generalisable to males as he used only female participants. However supporting studies have used males as well as females.

- Majority influence appears to be an unthinking, immediate force that maintains the status quo (keeps things as they are) therefore helping to resist social change. However, minority influence is a slower acting force, requiring active, private consideration of a minority's viewpoint which leads gradually to majority acceptance and social change.

- Majority and minority influence both lead to behavioural changes but for different reasons and through different processes. Majority influence concerns a need for social acceptance through compliance, while minority influence concerns a need for innovation through social change.

Typical mistake

A common assumption that students make is that all the factors relating to how social influence research helps us to understand social change should be mentioned in an examination answer or they will lose marks. This is not the case. You can only gain marks for that which is creditworthy. The decision on how much information to include in your answer should be driven by how many marks are available.

Now test yourself

12 What is meant by independent behaviour?

13 Explain what is meant by dissent. What has research indicated about dissent as a form of independent behaviour?

14 Aside from dissent, what other factors are involved in resisting conformity?

15 Explain what is meant by the following factors involved in resisting obedience and give research evidence for each: (i) decreasing agentic state (ii) increasing personal responsibility (iii) systematic processing (iv) morality (v) experience (vi) personality.

16 What is meant by social change?

17 Explain how the promotion of group status can achieve positive social change.

18 Detail how the following can affect social change: (i) rebellious role models (ii) reversal of gradual commitment (iii) exposure to models of independent behaviour.

19 Give details of three studies that investigated the role of minority influence on social change.

Answers on p. 107

Exam practice

1 Complete the following table of descriptions by placing the correct social influence term next to the correct definition. One term will be left over. [4]

Informational social influence   Internalisation
Normative social influence   Minority influence
Obedience

Definition	Description
	Going along with the majority in the belief they are correct
	Looking to a group for guidance on how to behave
	Complying with the demands of an authority figure
	Conforming to group behaviour in order to fit in

2 Shalene has recently started work at a factory and would like to make some new friends. She has noticed that many of her co-workers are fans of Greensborough Town, the local football team, so she buys a replica team shirt and wears it to work.

Identify what type of conformity is illustrated in the description above. Refer to features of the situation to justify your answer. [1 + 2]

3 Outline and evaluate two ethical issues raised in Milgram's study of obedience. [3 + 3]

4 Discuss explanations of why people obey. [12]

5 Explain how locus of control can be used as an explanation of independent behaviour. [4]

6 Outline and evaluate the role of minority influence in social change. [12]

Answers and quick quiz 5 online

Examiner's summary

✔ Kelman identified different types of conformity, which vary in strength by the extent to which they affect belief systems.

✔ There are several types of conformity, which can be related to specific research studies (e.g. Asch to normative social influence and Jenness to informational social influence).

✔ Close reference to Milgram's work should be made to outline what is meant by obedience to authority and to explain reasons why people obey.

✔ Independent behaviour is explicable by reference to locus of control and to factors that assist resistance to conformity and obedience to authority, like dissent and decreasing the agentic state.

✔ Social influence research brings an understanding of social change, especially of how minority influence encourages innovation by altering attitudes and behaviour over time to incur fundamental changes in belief systems.

Exam practice answers and quick quizzes at **www.therevisionbutton.co.uk/myrevisionnotes**

6 Individual differences — psychopathology (abnormality)

Definitions of abnormality

The state of **abnormality** is difficult to define, as psychologists disagree over its causes and how it displays itself. Some see abnormality as resulting from defective biology, others from 'incorrect' learning, faulty cognitive processes or problems of the mind and personality. Different views of abnormality dominate at different times and in different cultures.

> **abnormality** — a psychological or behavioural state leading to impairment of interpersonal functioning

Rosenhan and Seligman (1995) define abnormality as 'an absence of normality', therefore by defining abnormality, we make judgements about what is 'normal'. Several criteria for abnormality have been proposed, each with its own strengths and weaknesses.

Examiner's tip

The specification requires that candidates know the limitations of definitions of abnormality. One limitation worth knowing in detail, as it can be applied to all definitions, is that of cultural relativity, the idea that no universal definition of abnormality exists applicable to all cultures and that therefore individuals should not be judged by another culture's definition of abnormality.

Deviation from social norms

Each society has its own 'norms' (expected forms of acceptable behaviour). **Deviation from social norms** is perceived as being abnormal. Abnormality is therefore defined as 'behaviour that violates social norms'.

> **deviation from social norms** — behaviour violating accepted social rules

This definition gives a social dimension to abnormality, with the exclusion from society of those seen as behaving in socially unacceptable ways. The criteria are based upon the concept of social deviance, abnormal individuals being classed as social deviants thus allowing a distinction between desirable and undesirable behaviours. Using criteria to identify social deviants permits clinical interventions to help them achieve 'normality'. Such interventions are often beneficial, as some individuals (e.g. sexual deviants) may be unable to identify their problems and seek help themselves.

Limitations of the definition

- Individuals who do not conform to society's norms may merely be individualistic or eccentric and not abnormal in any problematic sense to themselves or anyone else.

- Violation of social norms may just be an excuse used by influential groups to intervene in the lives of non-conformists seen as challenging such groups' influential positions in society. For example, some countries have labelled political opponents as abnormal and confined them to mental institutions.

- Social deviancy is related to a particular culture's ideas about morality; this is a subjective judgement and will vary according to social attitudes. A true definition of abnormality should be unbiased and objective and thus unchanging across different cultures.
- An individual's behaviours and characteristics are usually judged in terms of the dominant culture's social norms, without reference to the norms of the individual's culture of origin. This makes the definition *culturally relative*, as it relates only to one particular culture's view of social norms.

> **Typical mistake**
>
> A common mistake students make when asked to explain one limitation of a particular definition is to identify several limitations without giving any details. Examiners would only give credit for the best one and without elaboration this is likely to receive a maximum of 1 mark. Rather than learning long lists of limitations, a much better policy is to learn a few but in considerable depth.

Failure to function adequately

Revised ☐

This definition sees individuals as abnormal when their behaviour suggests that they cannot cope with everyday life.

Sue et al. (1994) reported that the majority of people seeking clinical help feel they are suffering from psychological problems that obstruct their ability to function adequately. Behaviour is considered abnormal when it causes distress leading to dysfunction, like disrupting the ability to work and/or conduct satisfactory interpersonal relationships.

The definition focuses on individual suffering, concentrating on the personal experiences associated with mental disorders. It is therefore an *individualistic* or *humanistic* one, as it permits individuals to decide if they are abnormal, though others can also judge if a person is not coping.

Rosenhan and Seligman (1989) suggest that personal dysfunction has seven features. The more features an individual shows, the more they are classed as abnormal (see Table 6.1).

> **failure to function adequately** — inability to cope with day-to-day living

> **Examiner's tip**
>
> A popular question about the 'failure to function adequately' definition of abnormality would be to ask candidates to complete a table of features of personal dysfunction. A good way of preparing for such a question would be to compile and learn the features and to test yourself on knowledge of it.

Table 6.1 Features of personal dysfunction

Features of personal dysfunction	Description of feature
Personal distress	A key feature of abnormality that includes depression and anxiety disorders
Maladaptive behaviour	Behaviour that prevents realisation of life goals, both socially and occupationally
Unpredictability	Displaying unexpected behaviours characterised by loss of control, such as attempting suicide after losing your job
Irrationality	Displaying behaviour not explicable in a rational way
Observer discomfort	Displaying behaviour that causes discomfort to others
Violation of moral standards	Displaying behaviour that breaks expected ethical norms
Unconventionality	Displaying behaviour that does not conform to accepted rules or standards

Limitations of the definition

- An individual's behaviour may cause others distress and thus be perceived as dysfunctional, while the individual themself feels little or no distress.

- An individual's apparently dysfunctional behaviour may actually be rewarding. For example, a person's eating disorder can bring attention and sympathy from others.

- Not being able to cope with everyday life may be the cause of mental problems rather than an effect. Ethnic minorities often experience elevated rates of mental disorders due to the high levels of everyday social stressors they have to contend with.

- Definitions of 'inadequate functioning' vary from culture to culture. Therefore we should not use what's considered inadequate in our own culture to judge others of different cultural and sub-cultural backgrounds.

Deviation from ideal mental health

Revised ☐

This definition assesses abnormality in the same way that physical health is assessed, by searching for signs of an absence of well-being. Marie Jahoda (1958) proposed the concept of ideal mental health, identifying six categories of behaviour that a person should display in order to be seen as normal (see Table 6.2). Therefore an absence of these criteria indicates individuals to be abnormal.

As with other definitions, the focus is on desirable rather than undesirable behaviours and characteristics. The more criteria a person fails to meet and the further they are from realising individual criteria, the more abnormal they are. This definition has a positive emphasis on positive achievements rather than failures and distress.

> **deviation from ideal mental health** — failure to meet the criteria for perfect psychological well-being

Table 6.2 Criteria of ideal mental health

Criteria of ideal mental health	Description of criteria
Positive attitude towards oneself	Having self-respect and a positive self-concept
Self-actualisation	Experiencing personal growth. 'Becoming everything one is capable of becoming'
Autonomy	Being independent, self-reliant and able to make personal decisions
Resisting stress	Having effective coping strategies and being able to cope with everyday anxiety-provoking situations
Accurate perception of reality	Perceiving the world in a non-distorted fashion. Having an objective and realistic world view
Environmental mastery	Being competent in all aspects of one's life and able to meet the demands of any situation. Having the flexibility to adapt to changing life-circumstances

> **Typical mistake**
>
> Questions on the limitations of definitions of abnormality are usually worth 3 marks but many candidates, even though they have a good working knowledge of limitations, will give incomplete answers worth only 1 mark. The solution is to identify a valid limitation and provide further elaboration (e.g. by explaining the limitation to show understanding and/or giving a real life example to show the limitation's effect).

Limitations of the definition

- As it would be difficult to achieve all six criteria simultaneously, most people would be judged abnormal at a given moment in time. The criteria may therefore actually be **ideals** rather than **actualities**.
- Jahoda's criteria are vague and thus difficult to measure. Measurements of physical health tends to use objective tests, like x-rays, while diagnosing mental health is more subjective and reliant upon self-reports from individuals who may be mentally disordered and thus unreliable.
- Western cultures are orientated to individual goals and needs while collectivist cultures emphasise communal goals and behaviours and do not therefore view autonomy as desirable. This suggests that the criteria of autonomy only applies to Western cultures.
- The criteria used to judge mental health are culturally bound (specific to one culture) and should not be used to assess people of other cultural and sub-cultural groupings. *Koro* is one such culture-bound disorder, found in South-East Asia, China and Africa, where male sufferers believe their penis is retracting into their body.

Now test yourself

Tested

1 Outline the main features of the following definitions of abnormality: (i) deviation from social norms (ii) failure to function adequately (iii) deviation from ideal mental health.
2 Explain two limitations of each definition.
3 What is meant by the term cultural relativism?
4 Explain how all three definitions of abnormality can be seen as culturally relative.

Answers on p. 108

The biological approach

The biological model

Revised

The **biological model**, also known as the **medical model**, sees abnormality as mental illnesses caused by malfunctioning biological processes, specifically in the structure and workings of the brain, the nervous system, genetic influences and the biological environment.

The medical model has, in Western cultures, dominated the field of mental health for 200 years, giving rise to the dominant beliefs and practices of **psychiatry**, which sees mental illnesses (just like physical illnesses) as (1) having common groups of symptoms, (2) being separate from each other, (3) having physical causes and (4) being treated and cured by physical means.

Psychiatrists use diagnostic criteria for identifying mental illnesses, matching symptoms to classification systems. British psychiatrists use the *International Classification of Diseases — 10th edition* (ICD-10), while American psychiatrists use the *Diagnostic and Statistical Manual of Mental Disorders, 4th edition* (DSM-IV).

biological model — perceiving mental disorders as illnesses with physical causes

psychiatry — branch of medicine dealing with the study, diagnosis and treatment of mental illness

Several physical factors have been suggested as explanations of mental illnesses (see Table 6.3), for example abnormal levels of hormones and neurotransmitters (see page 66) can result in mental illness. Such factors often interact, for example Alzheimer's disease is associated with brain damage and genetic influences.

Table 6.3 Physical factors of mental illness

Physical factors of mental illness	Description of factors
Brain damage	Abnormal behaviour can result from physical brain damage. Alzheimer's disease, leading to memory loss, is caused by destruction of cells in the nervous system
The biological environment	Bacterial infections and viruses can also damage the brain, causing malfunctions. General paresis results from sexually contracted syphilis that damages the brain and leads to delusions, bizarre behaviours and finally death
Biochemistry	Faulty biochemistry, such as abnormal levels of hormones and neurotransmitters, can result in mental illness. High levels of dopamine are associated with schizophrenia
Genetics	Certain genes are linked to increased risk of developing mental illnesses. For example, research suggests a genetic link to the development of depression

Tien et al. (1990) reported that heavy and prolonged abuse of cocaine and/or amphetamines can lead to brain damage, resulting in psychosis. Symptoms include hallucinations, delusions, thought disorders and personality changes.

Hideyo & Moore (1913) found the syphilis bacterium in brain tissue samples taken from patients who had died from the degenerative mental disorder, paresis. This suggests that the biological environment can cause mental illness.

Janowsky (2009) found a link between abnormal neurotransmitter levels and the development of depression and manic depression. High levels of acetylcholine were associated with depression and low levels with mania. This suggests that biochemical imbalances can result in mental illness.

Weinberger et al. (2002) found that an abnormal variant of the COMT gene on chromosome 22 was linked to a near doubled risk of developing schizophrenia, by depleting the frontal lobes of the brain of the neurotransmitter dopamine, leading to hallucinations and an inability to perceive reality. This implies a genetic link to mental illness and demonstrates how biological factors can interact, in this case through genetics and neurotransmitters.

Evaluation of the biological model – supporting points

- As an explanatory theory, it is based upon well-established scientific disciplines, like medicine and biochemistry, which gives the model trustworthiness, validity and acceptability.

- It focuses on objectively measurable physiological features in the study, diagnosis and treatment of mental disorders. For example, both genes and brain chemistry can be manipulated and accurately measured to determine their effects. This allows clear, unbiased judgements to be made about causes of mental illnesses and the physical effects of treatments.

- It has contributed immensely to the creation of effective treatments and therapies. For example, drug therapies that suppress the effects of schizophrenia have had a significant impact on the lives of sufferers, allowing many schizophrenics to live relatively normal lives outside

Typical mistake

An easy trap to fall into when answering a question that calls for an outline of the biological *approach* is to outline aspects of biological *therapies* instead (e.g. drug treatments and ECT). Although these therapies are based upon the biological approach, describing them will not be creditworthy unless the underlying principles behind the biological approach are also clearly outlined.

a mental institution. This has had a knock-on effect in reducing the negative perception of schizophrenics that many of the general public held (though many still do hold media-generated negative viewpoints).

- It can be argued to be a humane approach, because it does not see sufferers as responsible for their actions, as they are ill. However, Szasz (1972) argues that the approach is actually inhumane, as a diagnosis of being mentally ill carries with it a stigma (negative label), which negatively affects the perception of sufferers by others and is difficult to get rid of, incurring long-term negative consequences, such as reduced employment prospects.

- Research suggests that the model's belief in distinct types of mental conditions based on diagnostic categories is a valid assumption (i.e. that separate forms of mental illness, such as schizophrenia, do exist and they are diagnosable by reported symptoms).

Evaluation of the biological model – non-supporting points

- The model is impoverished and simplistic in over-focusing upon physical symptoms, thus neglecting the role of underlying psychological factors (e.g. an individual's emotional experiences).

- Concordance rates for mental disorders between MZ (identical) twins are never 100%, which they would be if biology was solely responsible. The **diathesis-stress model** addresses this by proposing that individuals have different genetic susceptibilities to disorders, but that such disorders only develop with certain levels of stressful environments.

- Physical abnormalities associated with the model may actually be effects of mental disorders rather than causes. For instance, far from actually precipitating the disorder, the enlarged ventricles seen in the brains of some schizophrenics may actually result from their suffering the condition long term.

- Szasz (1962) argues that the mind does not exist in a physical sense and so cannot be diseased, suggesting the concept of 'mental illness' to be a myth. He believes the diagnosis of mental illness is a means of 'socially controlling' undesirable elements of society.

- Because physical treatments based upon the model (e.g. ECT and drugs) are effective, this lends support to the idea of abnormal conditions having a biological cause. However, the concept of **treatment aetiology fallacy** argues that it is a mistaken notion to believe the success of a treatment reveals the cause of a disorder.

> **Examiner's tip**
>
> When asked to provide evaluation in your answers, especially in the 'long-answer' 12-mark questions, a good way to access the higher mark bands is to construct evaluation that is 'balanced'. This is best achieved by providing a mixture of positive and negative points. So, for example, if asked to evaluate the biological approach, try to provide a combination of supportive and non-supportive points to show the model's strengths and weaknesses.

Psychological approaches

Psychological models see the origins of mental problems in abnormal thought patterns, emotional responses and behaviours, rather than in biology. They occur in three broad perspectives, (1) **psychodynamic model**, (2) **behavioural model**, and (3) **cognitive model**, each with a different explanation for the causes of abnormality and with different forms of treatments based upon their central beliefs.

> **psychodynamic model** — a psychological approach perceiving mental disorders as arising from unresolved, unconscious childhood disorders
>
> **behavioural model** — a psychological approach perceiving mental disorders as learned abnormal behaviours
>
> **cognitive model** — a psychological approach perceiving mental disorders as due to negative thoughts and illogical beliefs

Exam practice answers and quick quizzes at **www.therevisionbutton.co.uk/myrevisionnotes**

Psychodynamic model

Revised

Associated with Freud, the psychodynamic model attempts to explain the motivating forces behind behaviour and perceives abnormality as occurring due to unconscious, unresolved childhood traumas.

Freud saw personality as consisting of three parts, the id, the ego and the super-ego. The ego attempts to balance out the clash between the id's desire for immediate gratification and the super-ego's desire for constant morality. When this balance is not achieved, anxiety results. The ego uses **defence mechanisms** to attempt to deal with anxiety, like **repression** (where threatening thoughts are hidden in the unconscious mind), **displacement** (where anger is directed elsewhere), **projection** (where someone else is blamed), **denial** and **regression** (where an individual acts like a child).

Special importance is placed on the first five years of life where children progress through stages of **psychosexual development**. Unresolved traumas during these stages are repressed into the unconscious mind, but can affect adult conscious behaviour as fixations or manifest themselves as physical illnesses.

> **Williams (1994)** found that 38% of women reportedly abused as children could not recall the abuse, especially if it was by someone they knew. This suggests repression of traumatic events, supporting psychodynamic theory.
>
> **Solms (2000)** used PET scans on non-brain-damaged individuals to strengthen Ito's (1998) claim that the id is located in the limbic system, while the ego and super-ego are in the frontal lobes of the cerebral cortex, giving clinical support to psychoanalytic theory.

defence mechanisms — tactics developed by the ego to protect against anxiety

repression — unconscious exclusion of painful desires, fears and memories

Typical mistake

Psychology relies heavily upon research studies, but often students fail to use research evidence in the most creditworthy way and instead provide inappropriate details. Unless answering a question where specific description of a study's aims, procedures etc is called for, the best policy is to say what was found (results) and what this means in terms of the point being made. Using phrases like 'this suggests...' or 'this implies...' is a good way to achieve this.

Evaluation of psychodynamic theory

- The model removes responsibility for abnormality from the patient, as the behaviour is seen as coming from the unconscious mind. Indeed blame is often allocated to parents and carers.

- Empirical evidence supports the idea of mentally disordered patients having earlier conflicts, with Barlow and Durand (1995) finding that childhood traumas can result in adult abnormality.

- The original model over-emphasised childhood influences at the expense of adult ones and over-emphasised sexual factors due to the sexually constrained times in which Freud lived. Current psychodynamic theorists acknowledge this and recognise the role that inadequate interpersonal relationships and everyday problems play in abnormality.

- The model puts blame onto poor parenting, child abuse cases being used to support this claim. However false memory syndrome (see page 98) shows how 'recovered' memories of abuse are often phony and are generated by therapists' suggestive questioning techniques. The use of recovered memories is now banned in psychotherapy.

Behavioural model of abnormality

Revised

The behavioural model focuses on observable, measurable behaviour rather than on hidden mental processes, with maladaptive (abnormal) behaviour seen as occurring through the learning processes of (1) **classical conditioning**, (2) **operant conditioning** and (3) **social learning**.

Classical conditioning

Classical conditioning works on reflex actions where a neutral stimulus acquires the properties of another stimulus through association. Phobias (irrational fears) can be learned by an object or situation becoming associated with a fear response, while sexual fetishes can be similarly learned where an object or situation becomes paired with an arousal response.

Operant conditioning

Operant conditioning involves learning through the consequences of behaviour, where if behaviour is **reinforced** (rewarded) it is maintained or increased and if punished, ceases.

Abnormal behaviour can occur through operant conditioning. For example, losing weight can attract praise from others, which is positively reinforcing, motivating an individual to lose further weight, which can ultimately result in an eating disorder. A disorder which seemingly incurs a negative outcome for a sufferer may actually be reinforcing, for instance depression may bring extra attention and sympathy from others, increasing the likelihood of the condition being maintained or increased.

Social learning theory

Social learning theory (SLT) sees the development of abnormal behaviours occurring through **vicarious learning**, where a role model who exhibits a behaviour, and is seen to be rewarded for it, is observed and imitated.

SLT explains the acquisition of an eating disorder as forming through the observation and imitation of a highly regarded person. Similarly, drug addiction could be initiated through the imitation of drug-taking habits by peers seen to attract favourable attention from others for their behaviour.

> **Krafft-Ebbing (1886)** reported on a man who developed masochistic sexual tendencies through accidental friction on his penis while being spanked as a child, which suggests that the fetish occurred by associating arousal with punishment in line with classical conditioning.
>
> **Wikler (1973)** reported how drug addiction is maintained through operant conditioning, with drug-taking being negatively reinforced through termination of cravings.
>
> **Mineka et al. (1984)** reported how young monkeys learned snake phobias by observing older monkeys exhibit fear in the presence of snakes, supporting the idea of phobias being acquired through social learning.

Evaluation of the behavioural model

- The model is sensitive to individual differences and social and cultural contexts, as the specific behavioural history of patients is acknowledged as shaping their maladaptive behaviour.
- The model does not label sufferers with the damaging, long-lasting stigma of being 'ill'. Instead mental disorders are seen purely as maladaptive responses, changeable through relearning to become adaptive and correct.

classical conditioning — a method of learning where innate reflexes become paired with other stimuli through repeated association

operant conditioning — a method of learning where the likelihood of a behaviour occurring is increased or decreased through the use of rewards

social learning — a method of learning occurring through observation and imitation of others

Exam practice answers and quick quizzes at **www.therevisionbutton.co.uk/myrevisionnotes**

- The model over-emphasises external environmental factors at the expense of internal biological factors and therefore cannot explain disorders with clear biological elements, such as schizophrenia.
- The model is reductionist in perceiving abnormality as due only to learning, with many disorders being more complex than this (e.g. those with a cognitive element that the model does not consider).

The cognitive model of abnormality

Revised

The cognitive model resembles the behavioural model in acknowledging the role of maladaptive learning but also considers the role of internal mental processes, perceiving mental disorders as due to maladaptive thought processes (negative thoughts and irrational beliefs) referred to as **cognitive errors**, which exert influence over emotions and behaviour leading to abnormality.

Individuals with mental problems tend to have **negative automatic thoughts** (pessimistic thoughts that occur without conscious consideration), make inaccurate **attributions** when making sense of their own and others' behaviour and have illogical expectations (e.g. expecting relationships to end in failure).

The model sees disordered people as lacking confidence to achieve life-goals, with maladaptive thought processes leading to maladaptive behaviour. For example Beck (1963) proposed the **cognitive triad** (see Table 6.4), three illogical thought processes which lead to irrational, negative emotions and depression.

> **cognitive triad** — the three types of illogical thought processes that result in irrational, negative feelings, which can lead to depression

Table 6.4 Components of the cognitive triad

Components of the cognitive triad	Examples of the components
Negative self-feelings	'Nobody loves me'
Negative feelings about the future	'I will always be useless'
Negative views about oneself	'I have no value'

Gustafson (1992) found that patients suffering from depression, anxiety disorders and sexual problems often displayed maladaptive thinking, supporting the idea of a cognitive component to abnormality.

Abela & D'Alessandro (2002) found that students at risk of developing depression due to dysfunctional attitudes who didn't get into their preferred universities subsequently doubted their academic abilities, with such thoughts then leading to depression, suggesting a cognitive link to depression.

Armfield (2007) asked participants to visualise a spider in varying conditions of danger and controllability, finding that participants who believed they could not escape and that the spider was dangerous and unpredictable in its movements scored more highly on fear of spiders, which implies that individual beliefs determine vulnerability to anxiety, thus supporting the cognitive model.

Evaluation of the cognitive model

- The model has been influential, especially when combined with the behavioural model to form the cognitive-behavioural model.

- Research has found that many sufferers of anxiety disorders and depression do report irrational thought processes, giving support to the cognitive explanation of abnormality.
- The model has a positive approach in empowering individuals, by perceiving them as having personal ability to change their maladaptive cognitions for the better.
- It is not clear whether irrational thought processes are the causes of mental disorders, or merely the effects of them.
- The model is somewhat reductionist in perceiving individuals as responsible for their maladaptive thoughts and behaviour, thus ignoring the important role of situational factors (e.g. an individual's life events) and biological factors (e.g. genetics) which may contribute to some mental disorders.
- Rather than being cognitively irrational, depressives may actually may have a more realistic perception of life than 'normal' people. Viewing life through 'rose-tinted spectacles' might be irrational, but it is psychologically healthy.

Now test yourself

Tested ☐

5 Outline the biological model of abnormality.
6 What evidence is there that the following factors can cause mental illness: (i) infections/viruses (ii) biochemistry (iii) genetics (iv) brain damage?
7 Outline how the following psychological models see mental disorders as arising: (i) psychodynamic model (ii) behavioural model (iii) cognitive model.

Answers on p. 108

Biological therapies

The biological model perceives abnormalities as mental illnesses with physiological causes and thus sees cures as occurring through therapies that treat patients' physical symptoms. The two main **biological therapies** are drug treatment and electro-convulsive therapy (ECT).

> **biological therapies** — treatments of abnormality based on the biological model

Drug treatment

Revised ☐

Twenty-five percent of National Health Service (NHS) drugs are prescribed for mental health problems (**drug therapy**); £159 million, incorporating 5.2% of the NHS budget, was spent on them in 1992–93.

> **drug therapy** — treatment of mental disorders with medicines

Psychiatric drugs reach the brain by entering the bloodstream to modify behavioural effects by increasing or decreasing the availability of neurotransmitters (chemical messengers in the nervous system), the main ones being dopamine, serotonin, acetylcholine, noradrenaline and GABA. **Antagonists** are drugs blocking the effects of neurotransmitters, while **agonists** are those mimicking or increasing neurotransmitter effects.

There are five main types of psychiatric drugs (see Table 6.5).

Table 6.5 Types of psychiatric drugs

Types of drugs	Description
Anti-manic drugs (mood stabilisers)	e.g. Lithium. Treats manic depression and severe depression by calming over-stimulated brain areas
Anti-depressant drugs	e.g. Prozac. Reduces low moods and depressive symptoms by increasing production of serotonin. Three types: (i) Tricyclic antidepressants (TCAs) — increase noradrenaline levels (ii) Monoamine oxidase inhibitors (MAOIs) — increase noradrenaline levels by a different method (iii) Selective serotonin re-uptake inhibitors (SSRIs) — increases serotonin levels
Anti-anxiety drugs	e.g. Valium. Treats stress symptoms and short-term management of phobias by slowing activity of central nervous system
Anti-psychotics	e.g. Chlorpromazine. Combats schizophrenic symptoms, mania and psychosis by lowering dopamine activity. Two types: (i) First generation (typical) — stops dopamine production (ii) Second generation (atypical) — acts upon dopamine and serotonin levels
Stimulants	e.g. Methylphenidate. Improves mood, alertness and confidence by triggering release of noradrenaline and dopamine

Furukawa et al. (2003), reviewing 35 studies, found that antidepressants were more effective than placebos (dummy pills), which implies antidepressants to be appropriate for treating depression.

Bergqvist et al. (1999) found that low doses of the anti-psychotic drug Risperidone were effective in treating obsessive-compulsive disorder (OCD), due to the drug's dopamine-lowering effect.

Kahn et al. (2008) found first generation anti-psychotics to be effective for at least one year in treating symptoms of first-episode schizophrenia, but that second generation drugs were no more effective. This suggests that first generation anti-psychotics are superior as, being cheaper, they are more cost-effective.

Evaluation of drug treatments

- Drugs are relatively cost-effective, easy to administer and are favoured by patients, as they are familiar with and have confidence in taking them.

- Evidence supports the effectiveness of drugs. Anti-psychotics work for 65% of psychotic patients and 80% of schizophrenics.

- Although drugs do not 'cure' but simply reduce symptoms, such symptom reduction improves patients' lives, with 75% of depressives using appropriate drugs remaining depression free for extended periods.

- Drugs can incur unpleasant and dangerous side-effects as they interfere with brain mechanisms other than those associated with mental disorders. For example, anti-psychotics can damage the immune system and Valium is addictive.

- Drugs may address the effects of mental disorders but not necessarily the causes. Thus, once treatment ceases, disorders may return.

- In some mental institutions drugs are incorrectly used to control/ sedate patients rather than treat them. In such instances they have been nicknamed 'the chemical cosh' and 'pharmacological straitjackets'.

Electro-convulsive therapy

Electro-convulsive therapy (ECT) is used to treat depressive disorders, often those incurring a risk of suicide, although recently it has been re-introduced as a treatment for schizophrenia. It is mainly used when drugs and psychotherapy have failed or cannot be tolerated.

> **electro-convulsive therapy** — treatment of mental disorders by applying electrical voltages to the brain

Approximately 22,000 people a year receive ECT in Britain, with treatment given several times a week for between 6–12 treatments, with a general anaesthetic and a muscle-relaxant given before treatment so that patients do not feel pain or convulse and incur fractures. Brain stimulation occurs through electrodes placed on the head, with a brief, controlled series of electrical pulses of between 70–150 volts, causing a brain seizure lasting about one minute. After 5–10 minutes, the patient regains consciousness.

There are two types of ECT: **unilateral ECT**, involving stimulation of the non-dominant hemisphere of the brain and **bilateral ECT**, involving stimulation of both hemispheres.

Several explanations of how ECT works have been offered, with current thinking favouring the idea that ECT induces changes in neurotransmitter levels, including increased sensitivity to serotonin in the hypothalamus and an increase in the release of GABA, noradrenaline and dopamine.

> **Levy (1968)** compared bilateral and unilateral forms of electro-convulsive therapy as treatments of depression, finding that unilateral versions incurred less memory loss, but that bilateral versions provided more effective relief of depressive symptoms.
>
> **Pagnin et al. (2008)** performed a meta-analysis of studies comparing the effectiveness of electro-convulsive therapy, antidepressants and placebos in treating depression, finding ECT to be superior in treating severe and resistant forms of the disorder. This suggests ECT to be a valid therapeutic treatment.
>
> **Comer (2002)** found that 70% of depressives improve after receiving electro-convulsive therapy. However, improvements seem short-lived, as Sackheim et al. (2001) found that 84% of depressives treated with ECT re-experience serious depression within 6 months of treatment. This suggests that ECT is only a short-term treatment and not a long-term solution for depression.
>
> **Tharyan & Adams (2005)**, reviewing studies of electro-convulsive therapy, found it a short-term effective treatment of schizophrenia, but not as effective as anti-psychotics, though Tang et al. (2000) found ECT to be effective in treating schizophrenics who did not respond positively to anti-psychotics. This suggests that ECT does have beneficial uses as a treatment of schizophrenia in some instances.

Evaluation of electro-convulsive therapy

- It saves lives, as severe depressives who are non-responsive to other treatments are at severe risk of committing suicide.

- Compared to drug treatments and psychological therapies, ECT is a relatively quick and cost-effective treatment.

- ECT generally has an immediate positive effect, while drugs can take considerable periods of time before improvements are noticeable, by which time the occurence of side-effects may mean patients have discontinued the treatment.

- There is no evidence that ECT is physically damaging. Coffey used MRI scans to find that ECT treatments did not incur brain damage in patients.

- ECT should only be used when other treatments have failed, but 18% of patients are not offered any other treatments and it is not perceived positively; UKAN (1995) reported that 78.5% of patients surveyed said they would not have the treatment again.

- It can cause memory loss, especially if bilateral, which builds up over treatment.

- Side-effects of ECT are more severe in children, the elderly, pregnant women and adolescents, which suggests the treatment is not suitable for many patients, unless as a last resort.

- There are ethical concerns with ECT usage as it can be a fairly frightening experience, with some patients perceiving it as 'punishment' for being mentally impaired. It is also debatable if severely depressed/ suicidal patients can comprehend enough to give informed consent. Many patients receive treatment without consent under the Mental Health Act.

Psychological therapies

The three main psychological therapies — (1) **psychodynamic**, (2) **behavioural** and (3) **cognitive** — treat mental disorders with therapies based upon their particular viewpoints as to what causes abnormality. Collectively they offer alternatives to the biological therapies. No one psychological therapy is best; each has strengths and limitations and each is more effective in particular instances.

> **psychological therapies** — treatment of mental disorders based on psychological rather than biological explanations

Psychoanalysis   Revised ☐

As the psychodynamic model sees mental disorders as resulting from unresolved conflicts, psychodynamic treatments attempt to identify the nature of a conflict and then resolve it. As conflicts are unconscious, psychotherapists use **psychoanalysis** (techniques like **dream analysis** and **free association**) to try to allow patients insight into the origins of their disorders so that they can achieve an understanding of repressed events that occurred in their past.

> **psychoanalysis** — a psychodynamic treatment of mental disorders seeking to give patients insight into the origins of disorders

Dream analysis

The images and events of dreams are seen as containing repressed thoughts and desires, which 'bubble up' during dreams as ego-defences are lowered, revealing inner conflicts through their symbolism and deeper meaning. The **manifest content** of a dream is what it appears to be about (such as bridge collapsing), while the **latent content** is the real meaning (such as anxiety about a failing relationship).

Free association

Patients are encouraged to 'free associate' (speak freely without reservation, contemplation or inhibition) thus revealing their 'stream of consciousness', which a trained analyst can then analyse to reveal inner conflicts. Therapists take care not to react in a critical fashion and look for signs of **resistance** (reluctance by patients to talk about a particular topic) which may reveal clues about an inner conflict.

> **Andreoli et al. (1999)** found psychodynamic psychotherapy, where patients relive childhood experiences, an effective treatment if delivered by skilled therapists, implying that treatment effectiveness is dependent on the quality of clinicians.

> **Leichsenring et al. (2004)** found brief dynamic therapy, a simplified form of psychoanalysis, as effective as cognitive-behavioural therapy in treating depression. As CBT is the prime treatment for depression, this gives considerable support to the therapy.

Typical mistake

A common mistake when evaluating psychoanalysis is to provide general criticisms of Freud's theory. Much more creditworthy is to give evaluative points that are specific to psychoanalysis (this point also relates to evaluation of the psychodynamic explanation of abnormality).

Evaluation of psychoanalysis

- Although psychoanalysis seems inappropriate for disorders with a biological component, like schizophrenia, psychoanalysis has proven effective in treating certain psychological abnormalities, like anxiety disorders.

- Modern forms of psychoanalysis occur over a shorter time-span and concentrate more on current issues, producing swifter results and proving more cost-effective.

- Ethical concerns are raised with psychoanalysis as it can involve reliving painful events and may produce **false memory syndrome**, with patients recalling 'repressed' memories which are false, occurring through suggestive therapeutic techniques.

- Psychoanalysis is based upon Freudian theory, criticised for its lack of scientific evidence. Dream analysis and free association cannot be empirically tested and are based on analysts' subjective interpretations.

Systematic de-sensitisation

Revised ☐

Systematic de-sensitisation (SD) is a behaviourist therapy designed by Wolpe (1958) to counteract phobias, with behaviourism perceiving phobias as arising from the irrational fears experienced in response to certain objects or situations (e.g. being scared of snakes).

The central idea of SD is that it is impossible to experience the two opposite emotions of fear and relaxation simultaneously, so SD uses classical conditioning to gradually replace irrational fears with the incompatible response of relaxation. Patients are taught deep muscle relaxation strategies and use these in rising stages of intensity (from weakest to strongest) when faced with the phobic object/ situation. For example, a snake phobic would first look at a picture of a snake, then at a snake in a tank and so on until finally holding a snake without experiencing fear. This is achieved by using relaxation strategies and only moving onto the next stage when a relaxed state is maintained.

systematic de-sensitisation — a behavioural therapy that modifies phobias by constructing and working through a hierarchy of anxiety-producing stimuli

Examiner's tip

Some psychological terms, like systematic de-sensitisation, are time-consuming to have to write out several times in an examination answer. A good strategy is to abbreviate such terms. The accepted way of doing this is to write the term out in the first instance (e.g. 'systematic de-sensitisation') followed immediately by the abbreviation (e.g. SD) and then just to use the abbreviation after that.

Klosko et al. (1990) compared various therapies for the treatment of panic attacks, finding 87% patients panic free after systematic de-sensitisation, 50% after taking the drug Alprazolam, 36% with a placebo and 33% with no treatment. This suggests that SD is highly effective.

Jones (1924) used systematic de-sensitisation to eradicate 'Little Peter's' phobia of white fluffy objects by presenting a white rabbit at ever closer distances each time the boy's anxiety levels lessened. Eventually he was content in the presence of the rabbit, a feeling which generalised to similar white, fluffy objects.

Evaluation of systematic de-sensitisation

- SD, like behavioural therapies in general, is quick to administer and requires less input from patients than other psychological therapies.

- It is less traumatic than other behavioural treatments, such as flooding, where phobias are confronted directly and immediately. SD is a much more gentle step-by-step approach and as such can be argued to be more ethical.

- It is not effective in treating innate phobias that have an evolutionary origin. Such phobias have a survival element to them, have not been developed through environmental experience and thus cannot be removed by conditioning techniques.

- SD can often appear to have eradicated a particular phobia, only for the patient to develop a different phobia in another area of personal functioning. This phenomenon is known as **symptom substitution** and suggests that SD is merely addressing the effects of a psychological problem, not its causes.

Cognitive-behavioural therapy
Revised

Cognitive-behavioural therapy (CBT) is based on the cognitive model which sees abnormality as arising from disordered thought processes. CBT is a general term, encompassing a number of different therapies, the best known being **rational emotive behaviour therapy** (REBT).

> **cognitive-behavioural therapy** — challenging and restructuring abnormal ways of thinking into useful, rational ones

Rational emotive behaviour therapy

Devised by Ellis (1975), rational emotive behaviour therapy sees irrational thoughts as causing emotional distress and behaviour disorders, involving the use of **negative self-statements**, with therapy aiming to make these statements more rational and positive. Ellis (1990) identified 11 basic irrational, emotionally damaging '**mustabatory beliefs**' that lead to psychological problems (e.g. 'I must be perfect in all respects').

Patients are encouraged to practise positive modes of thinking using the **ABC technique**, which comprises three steps, analysing how irrational beliefs are developed (see Table 6.6). REBT ultimately involves **reframing** — challenging negative thoughts by reinterpreting the ABC technique in a more positive, logical way (e.g. 'enough time was not created for revision' instead of 'I'm stupid').

Table 6.6 ABC technique steps

ABC technique steps	Description
A = Activating event	Patients record events leading to disordered thinking e.g. exam failure
B = Beliefs	Patients record negative thoughts associated with the event e.g. 'I'm useless and stupid'
C = Consequence	Patients record negative thoughts/behaviours that occur e.g. feeling upset/wanting to leave college

Kvale et al. (2004) performed a meta-analysis of treatment studies for patients with dental phobias, finding that 77% of patients regularly visited a dentist four years after treatment, implying the treatment to be effective.

Tarrier (2005) reported cognitive-behavioural therapy to be an effective treatment of schizophrenia, finding evidence of reduced symptoms and lower relapse rates.

Evaluation of cognitive-behavioural therapy

- Research suggests that CBT is useful in addressing a wide range of mental disorders (e.g. obsessive-compulsive disorder, post-traumatic stress disorder, social phobias). The Royal College of Psychiatrists sees it as the most effective treatment of moderate and severe depressions.

- It is particularly useful, as it is used with patients suffering from clinical mental disorders as well as those with moderate problems like nervousness.

- CBT is difficult to evaluate. Senra and Polaino (1998) found that assessing CBT with different measurement scales produced different rates of improvement among patients.

- It is dependent on patients being able to talk about thought processes coherently, not something that patients with severe mental impairments are always capable of.

Examiner's tip

A good way to create evaluation (aside from using support from research evidence), especially in 'long-answer' 12-mark questions, is to compare the effectiveness of different forms of therapy. So, for example, cognitive-behavioural therapy could be compared in terms of effectiveness with other psychological therapies (e.g. systematic de-sensitisation) and psychoanalysis and/or biological therapies (e.g. drugs and electro-convulsive therapy).

Now test yourself

Tested

8 How do drugs affect behaviour?

9 Give two pieces of research evidence that suggest drug treatments are effective.

10 What mental disorders is ECT used to treat?

11 Outline the procedure for ECT usage.

12 Give two pieces of research evidence that suggests ECT is effective.

13 Explain how the following psychological therapies treat mental disorders: (i) psychoanalysis (ii) systematic desensitisation (iii) CBT.

14 For each of these treatments give two pieces of research evidence that suggest they are effective.

Answers on p. 109

Exam practice

1 (a) Outline the deviation from mental health definition of abnormality. [4]

   (b) Explain one limitation of the (i) failure to function adequately and (ii) deviation from social norms definitions of abnormality. [2 + 2]

2 To what extent can the causes of abnormality be understood in terms of the biological model. [12]

3 Outline the main features of the psychodynamic approach to abnormality. [6]

4 Duncan has a phobia of dogs. Explain how Duncan's fear can be explained by the behaviourist model of abnormality. [4]

5 Explain one strength and one weakness of the cognitive model of abnormality. [2 + 2]

6 Helena has suffered for a long time with severe depression. Her condition has not responded to various treatments and she has been experiencing persistent suicidal thoughts. Her doctor has decided to give her ECT.

   (a) Explain why ECT might be an appropriate therapy for treating Helena. [3]

   (b) Outline one possible ethical consideration in giving ECT to Helena. [3]

7 Outline and evaluate two or more psychological treatments of abnormality. [12]

Answers and quick quiz 6 online

Online

Examiner's summary

✔ Several definitions of abnormality exist, all with limitations; a useful one to learn is cultural relativity, as it applies to all definitions.

✔ The biological approach sees abnormalities as mental illnesses explicable through malfunctioning biological processes, while psychological approaches perceive mental disorders arising through abnormal thought patterns, emotional responses and behaviour.

✔ Different approaches can be evaluated in terms of the degree to which research suggests they can explain individual mental disorders and by the success rates of treatments based upon each individual approach.

✔ Biological therapies treat physical symptoms, with evidence showing both drugs and ECT to be effective against various disorders, though both treatments incur side-effects.

✔ Psychological therapies are based upon different psychological approaches to understanding abnormality, with better prepared candidates being aware that no one psychological therapy is regarded as best as each has its own strengths and weaknesses and is more effective in particular circumstances.

✔ A useful means of building evaluation is achieved by comparing the effectiveness of different therapies, either through comparison with similar treatments, like different psychological ones, or through comparing treatments from different approaches, like psychological against biological ones.

Now test yourself answers

1 (i) the form in which information is stored (ii) amount of information that can be stored (iii) length of time information remains in storage.

2 STM — a temporary store holding small amounts of information for brief periods. LTM — a permanent store holding unlimited amounts of information for long periods. STM and LTM differ in terms of encoding, capacity and duration, as well as being associated with different brain areas.

3 Echoic store is for auditory information, iconic for visual.

4 *Positive:*

- MSM was influential, inspired research, led to other models being developed and a greater understanding of memory.

- Research supports the existence of separate memory stores.

- Amnesia studies suggest STM and LTM involve separate brain areas.

Negative:

- There are several stores in STM and LTM that the model does not acknowledge.

- The model over-emphasises memory structures at the expense of processes.

- Memory capacity is best understood by the nature of information, rather than quantity.

5 *Positive criticisms* — (i) the WMM does not over-emphasise the importance of rehearsal for STM retention (ii) PET scans support the idea of separate components.

Negative criticisms — (i) WMM only concerns STM and so is not a comprehensive model of memory (ii) little is known of the CE in terms of what it is and how it works.

6 Schemas are expectations of what is being perceived, based on previous experiences, moods, existing knowledge, stereotypes, contexts and attitudes. EWT can be biased by schemas active at the time of recall.

7 Research shows that leading questions affect schemas, and thus memory, and that at recall misleading information is reconstructed with material from original memories.

8 The inverted-U hypothesis argues that moderate amounts of anxiety improve the detail and accuracy of memory recall up to an optimal point, after which further increases in anxiety leads to a decline in recall.

9 Repression suggests that anxiety impairs recall of memories, with forgetting motivated by traumatic memories. Access to memories is denied in order to protect from emotional distress.

10 Research suggests that young children are vulnerable to leading questions and are especially misled by post-event information, leading to inaccurate EWTS. Accuracy of recall declines with age, with elderly witnesses susceptible to misleading information.

11 The cognitive interview is a police interview procedure to facilitate accurate, detailed recall.

12 (i) Change of narrative order — recount the scene in different chronological orders (ii) Change of perspective — recount the scene from different perspectives (iii) Mental reinstatement of context — return to both the environmental and emotional context of the crime scene (iv) Report everything — recall all information, even if appearing to have little relevance or is accorded a lower level of confidence.

13 (i) Retrieval cues are prompts triggering recall and occur as context-dependent cues, where similar external environments assist memory and state-dependent cues where a similar internal environment aids recall.

(ii) Chunking increases STM capacity by combining separate pieces of information into larger units with a common feature.

(iii) Mnemonics are memory aids that assist recall, usually by organisation of material, like structuring information to be remembered so that links are made to existing memories. Both visual and verbal techniques can be used.

(iv) Active processing refers to procedures that go beyond mere passive, unthinking encoding of information and instead subjects material to deep and meaningful processing.

Chapter 2

1 An attachment is a two-way emotional tie to a specific other person.

2 (i) Attachments form by classical conditioning through babies associating caregivers (conditioned reinforcer) with food (unconditioned reinforcer). (ii) Attachments form through operant conditioning by caregivers becoming associated with removing the unpleasant feeling of hunger and thus becoming a source of reinforcement.

3 Research generally does not support learning theory. Dollard and Miller (1950) calculate that carers feed babies 2,000 times in their first year, easily sufficient to learn an attachment, but many studies, such as Fox (1970), found that attachments are not always made to the main feeder.

4 Bowlby's theory of monotropy sees infants forming one prime bond to their main carer. This is an innate, evolved process with a survival value. Babies use inborn social releasers, like smiling and crying, to maintain parental attention and maintain a 'steady state' of physical proximity. Attachment behaviours function in an automatic, stereotyped manner, triggered initially by anyone. However over time they become focused on fewer individuals and organised into more flexible, sophisticated behaviour systems. Bowlby also envisages a critical period in which attachments must form or not form at all.

5 Lorenz (1935), who bonded goslings onto himself, supports the idea of attachment being a human form of imprinting. However other studies, like Rutter (1981), found babies develop multiple attachments to many people for many purposes, weakening the idea of monotropy.

6 (a) Secure — children are willing to explore, display high stranger anxiety, easy to soothe, enthusiastic at return of caregiver. Caregivers display sensitive responsiveness.

(b) Insecure–avoidant — children are willing to explore, display low stranger anxiety, indifferent to separation and avoid contact at the return of caregiver. Caregivers often ignore their charges.

(c) Insecure–resistant — children are not willing to explore, display high stranger anxiety, distress at separation and seek and reject contact at return of caregiver. Caregivers are ambivalent, displaying simultaneous opposite feelings and behaviours.

(d) Insecure–disorganised — displayed by a small number of children, whose behaviour is a confusing mixture of approach and avoidance behaviours.

7
- The strange situation is the paradigm, or accepted method of assessing attachments
- The finding that parental sensitivity determines attachment type has been supported by other research
- The strange situation is laboratory based and thus artificially assesses attachment and can be accused of lacking ecological validity
- The strange situation may be assessing individual relationships rather than general attachment patterns
- Some would argue the technique is unethical, as it stresses babies; others would argue the stress is no greater than normal life, such as leaving a baby with a babysitter

8
The strange situation may not be applicable in all cultures, like cultures where children are not left with strangers. Cultural childcaring styles need also to be considered when interpreting findings.

The strange situation is culture bound, as it only applies to Western cultural practices, such as regarding sociability in a positive manner.

In non-Western cultures children may be incorrectly assessed on the strange situation, which can have negative consequences, like being put into institutional care.

9
The MDH was formed from studies of institutionalised children and believes that if attachments are disrupted, serious irreversible damage will occur to emotional, social and intellectual capabilities.

10
Goldfarb (1943) compared institutionally raised and fostered children, finding that institutional care damaged social and intellectual development.

Bowlby (1944) found maternal separation incurs long-term, serious consequences, such as developing affectionless psychopathy where personality is characterised by no social conscience.

Spitz found disruption of attachment had negative outcomes, such as anaclitic depression, characterised by fear, social withdrawal, sadness, weight loss and developmental retardation.

11
PDD: protest, despair, detachment.

12 *STD*
- Robertson and Robertson (1971) found evidence of PDD with short-term hospitalisations, with long-term negative effects, such as tantrums.
- Douglas (1975) supported the MDH, finding separations of less than a week were associated with behavioural difficulties in children aged 4.
- Quinton and Rutter (1969) supported MDH, finding adolescent behavioural problems were related to short-term hospitalisations in the first 5 years of life.

LTD
- Schaffer (1996) found that most children are negatively affected by divorce.
- Hetherington and Stanley-Hagan (1999) found negative developmental outcomes due to divorce were more short than long term.
- Furstenberg and Kiernan (2001) found that children of divorced families score lower on measures of social development, emotional well-being, physical health and intellectual attainment.

13
Many children were placed in institutions before maternal bonds had formed and provided no opportunities for attachments to form.

14
- Privation is likelier than deprivation to incur lasting emotional damage, such as affectionless psychopathy.
- Tizard and Hodges (1978) found children who received institutional care had problems with peer relationships.
- Koluchova (1972) (1991) and Freud and Dann (1951) found that privation effects were reversible if sensitive, nurturing care was given over a long period.

15
Daycare refers to temporary care of children outside the home provided by non-family members, like in nurseries, but excludes institutional care.

16 *Against*
- Maternal separation results in deprivation, which damages social development.
- Homecare is superior to daycare in providing a more loving, stimulating environment.
- Homecare incurs superior social development.

For
- Daycare provides activities not available at home and interaction with others, both of which contribute to social development.
- High-quality daycare positively affects social development, with any negative effects due to poor quality provision.
- Daycare makes better mothers, as being free to work lowers stress and depression levels and increases self-esteem, allowing them to interact positively with their children.

17 *Aggression*
- There may be increased aggressiveness with daycare due to greater social interactions providing more opportunities for aggression to arise.
- Family features, like quality of home environment, are better indicators of aggressiveness than quantity of daycare received.
- Aggression in children is often confused with rough-and-tumble play, which can produce inaccurate indications of aggression levels associated with daycare.
- Daycare may not be responsible for heightened aggression, as aggressive children are more likely to be put into daycare by parents needing a break.

Peer relations
- Daycare has more opportunities for interaction and developing social skills, which leads to development of positive peer relationships.

- Daycare may harm the development of peer relations in children with low social competence and motor skills and provide opportunities for bullying by others.

18 Verbal interaction, stimulation, sensitive emotional care, low staff turnover, consistency of care, low staff–children ratio, mixed age groups, structured time.

19 • High quality daycare is required, as it has positive social developmental outcomes and thus is beneficial to society.

- Disadvantaged children should receive targeted high-quality daycare, as it benefits them most.

- Younger children should only attend daycare for short periods, which should be considered when formulating the workloads of returning-to-work mothers.

- Pre-assessment should occur, so that children vulnerable to negative outcomes can be identified and specially catered for.

- Childminders who are well-trained and offer high-quality care are as beneficial as good daycare provision.

- Working mothers are not associated with harming their children's social development, indeed working mothers have superior mental health and interact with their children more positively.

Chapter 3

1 (i) The variable manipulated by the researcher that changes between the conditions. (ii) A measurement of the effect of the IV.

2 Researchers keep all variables constant for all participants, except the IV.

3 Extraneous variables are variables other than the IV, which may affect the DV. If uncontrolled they can become confounding variables and confuse the results.

4 (i) Laboratory experiments occur in a controlled environment with a manipulated IV. (ii) Field experiments occur in a naturalistic setting with a manipulated IV. (iii) Natural experiments occur in a naturalistic setting with a naturally occurring IV.

5 The strength and direction of relationships between co-variables.

6 With a positive correlation, as the value of one co-variable increases so does the value of another. With a negative correlation, as the value of co-variable increases the value of another decreases.

7 Observations measure naturally occurring behaviour, but can also take place under controlled conditions. Participant observations involve the observers taking part in the behaviour, while non-participant observations involve merely watching behaviour. With overt observations participants are aware of being observed; with covert they are not.

8 With inter-rater reliability all observers measure and interpret behaviour in the same, consistent way. Agreed categories of behaviour are created and observers' observations are correlated with each other.

9 Questionnaires are a self-report method where respondents give written answers to pre-set questions.

10 Open questions allow freedom of expression, closed questions have fixed response options.

11 Interviews are a self-report method involving answering face-to-face questions. Structured interviews involve asking participants the same closed questions. Unstructured interviews involve informal discussion and permit follow-up questions. Semi-structured interviews involve a mixture of structured and unstructured techniques.

12 Case studies are in-depth studies of individuals or small groups of people.

13 Aims are precise statements of why investigations are occurring.

14 A testable prediction.

15 (i) Each participant does one condition. (ii) Each participant does all conditions. (iii) Participants are pre-matched into similar pairs, with one of each pair doing one condition each.

16 Asking relevant questions/keeping questionnaires short/ using successful questionnaires as a guide/using clear, concise, easily understandable questions/providing initial interesting questions to motivate participants to complete.

17 Interpersonal variables of interviewers e.g. age, gender etc. Training is also essential.

18 Defining variables simply and objectively in order to manipulate and measure them.

19 Pilot studies are small-scale practice investigations. They are conducted to identify and make necessary changes to the design and to see if meaningful results are likely to be found.

20 (i) Provide all necessary details so a considered decision can be made as to whether to participate. (ii) Do not withhold information or mislead participants. Use presumptive or prior general consent. (iii) Explain full relevant details and answer questions before and after an investigation. (iv) Risk of harm to be no greater than normal life. (v) Inform participants they can withdraw themselves and their data at any time. (vi) Use numbers instead of names. Only use data for agreed purposes. (vii) Only observe where people would expect to be observed.

21 (i) All members of a population have an equal chance of being selected, but representative samples are not guaranteed. (ii) Using whoever is available, though this can be unrepresentative. (iii) Using volunteers, though they are more prone to demand characteristics.

22 Demand characteristics are research effects where participants form impressions of the aim(s) and alter their behaviour accordingly. They can be reduced by using the single blind procedure.

23 Investigator effects are researcher features that influence participants' responses, such as primary and secondary physical characteristics and bias. They can be reduced by using a double-blind procedure.

24 Quantitative data occurs as numbers, while qualitative data is descriptive.

25 (i) Bar charts display data in the form of categories being compared. (ii) Histograms are used to present continuous data, like test scores. (iii) Frequency polygons also present continuous data and are used when two or more frequency distributions need to be compared. (iv) Scattergrams are used to display correlational data, showing how co-variables are related.

26 (i) The median is the middle score in a list of rank-ordered scores. (ii) The mean is the mathematical average, calculated by diving the total score by the number of scores. (iii) The mode is the most commonly occurring score in a set of data.

27 (i) The range shows the difference between the highest and lowest scores. (ii) The interquartile range shows the spread of the middle 50% of a set of scores. (iii) Standard deviation is a measure of the variability of a set of scores from the mean.

28 (i) Content analysis converts qualitative data into quantitative data, allowing the numerical analysis of written, verbal and visual communications, such as speeches, newspaper/ magazine articles, drawings and advertisements.

(ii) Content analysis requires the creation of quantifiable coding units to categorise material to be analysed. Categorising through coding units can involve words, themes, characters or time and space.

Chapter 4

1 The SMP deals with short-term acute stressors. The PAS deals with long-term chronic stressors.

2 SMP

- The SMP consists of the sympathetic nervous system (SNS) and the sympathetic adrenal medullary system (SAM).

- Acute stressors activate the two divisions of the autonomic nervous system (ANS): (i) the sympathetic nervous system (SNS), which responds to stressors and is responsible for emotional states and heightened arousal, and (ii) the parasympathetic nervous system (PNS), which maintains equilibrium and calms bodily processes.

- Acute stressors activate the SNS, while the SAM stimulates the release of noradrenaline from the adrenal glands in the adrenal medulla, preparing the body for 'flight or fight' by increasing oxygen and glucose supplies to the brain and muscles, while suppressing non-essential processes like digestion.

PAS

- Chronic stressors activate the PAS, with the hypothalamus stimulating the production of corticotrophin-releasing hormone (CRH).

- CRH activates the pituitary gland to release adrenocorticotrophic hormone (ACTH), which travels to the adrenal glands, triggering the release of the stress hormone cortisol.

- Cortisol elicits a steady supply of blood sugar to provide the body with a steady source of energy to combat stressors and tolerate elevated pain levels.

3 Acute stress produces the 'tend and befriend' response in women, but the 'flight or fight' response in men, as women produce more oxytocin, which produces nurturing and relaxation responses. This may have evolved due to women's role as childcarers.

4 The immune system protects the body against antigens by producing antibodies that bind to and destroy the antigens.

5 Prolonged stress reduces the immune system's ability to combat antigens, raising the risk of infection and illness. Continued production of cortisol reduces leucocyte activity and the production of antibodies, heightening the risk of infectious illness, such as influenza and chronic-fatigue disorder.

6 Kiecolt-Glaser et al. (1995) found chronic stress reduces immune system functioning, as wounds given to females who cared for senile parents took longer to heal than those without such stress.

Cohen et al. (1993) found stress creates greater vulnerability to illness, as stressed participants were more likely to catch a cold when exposed to the cold virus than non-stressed participants.

7 Life changes are occasional events incurring major adjustments to one's lifestyle.

8 Holmes and Rahe (1967) asked 100 judges to rate how stressful 43 common life changes were. These ratings formed the LCUs.

9 Holmes and Rahe (1967) found that individuals with high LCU scores for the past year had a heightened vulnerability to illness in the following year. Those with scores over 300 had an 80% risk of developing serious illnesses like cancer.

Rahe et al. (1972) supported the idea of a link between life changes and susceptibility to illness by finding a correlation between sailors' LCU scores and subsequent illness levels.

Li-Ping and Hammontree (1992) also suggested a link between life stress and illness by finding a relationship between police officers' stress levels and absenteeism.

10 Daily hassles are everyday irritations that produce an overall heightened level of stress, while life changes only occur occasionally.

11 Stressful life changes are rare. Most stress comes from the accumulation of daily hassles, like traffic jams, and thus are probably better indicators of health.

12 Van Houdenhove et al. (2002) found that certain people are more vulnerable, as chronic fatigue sufferers were more preoccupied with and affected by daily hassles than rheumatoid arthritis sufferers.

Sher (2004) reported that hassles increase stress hormone levels, as hassles were associated with heightened cortisol levels, which contribute to the onset of depression.

13 Workplace stressors are aspects of the work environment with a negative life impact. They can affect body response systems directly to lower health, such as through immunosuppression, or indirectly by encouraging unhealthy practices, like drinking.

14 Johansson et al. (1978) found that workers with workplace stressors like high workload, repetitiveness and high levels of responsibility had higher levels of stress hormones, stress-related illnesses and absenteeism.

Marmot et al. (1997) found that low job-control is harmful to health, as civil servants with low job-control were three times more vulnerable to heart attacks than those with high job-control.

Kivimaki et al. (2006) found that workplace stressors are related to illness as workers with high levels of job demand had heightened risk of heart attack.

Hobson and Beach (2000) found a cognitive element to workplace stressors, as psychological health in managers was related to individual perceptions of workload rather than actual workload.

15 Friedman and Rosenman (1974) found Type A personalities, characterised by impatience, ambitious competitiveness, frustration at goal blocking and aggressiveness under pressure, were more at risk of cardiovascular disorders.

Hayes (2000) found that particular Type A traits relate to specific cardiovascular disorders. Angina correlated with impatience and feeling pressurised by work, while heart attack patients were hasty in habits and schedules.

Matthews and Haynes (1986) supported Hayes' (2000) results, finding CHD was related to the Type A trait of hostility. Further support came from Forshaw (2002) finding hostility a better predictor of CHD than Type A personality as a whole.

16 Type C is a personality type characterised by suppression of negative emotions, incurring heightened risk of cancer. It's mainly associated with females and is characterised as being conventional, pleasant, caring and helpful to others.

Type D personality is a 'distressed' personality, characterised by worry, irritability, gloom, lack of sociability and a tendency to negative emotions that are revealed to others, due to a fear of rejection and disapproval. It is associated with heightened vulnerability to heart attacks.

17 Hardy personality is a healthy personality type characterised as having control over one's life, being committed to what one's doing and regarding stressors as enjoyable challenges that lead to self-improvement.

18 Kobasa (1979) found hardiness protects against stress-related illness, as stressed executives with high levels of hardiness had lower incidences of illness than those with low levels.

Dreher (1995) found that hardiness mediates the effects of stressors, as hardiness reduced illness by enhancing immune system functioning.

Maddi et al. (1998) found that hardiness can be learned, as managers receiving hardiness training had increased job satisfaction and decreased incidence of illness.

19 BZs are anti-anxiety drugs that dampen down nervous system activity, creating a sense of calm. The effect of the neurotransmitter GABA in suppressing neural activity is increased by stimulating an increase of chloride ions into brain neurons, making it difficult for other neurotransmitters to stimulate them. The excitatory effect of the neurotransmitter serotonin is also suppressed, adding to the calming effect.

BBs are anti-anxiety drugs that block the transmission of nerve impulses by 'sitting on' beta-adrenergic receptors, preventing them from being stimulated, reducing heart rate and lowering the physical, damaging effects of anxiety.

20 Havoundjian et al. (1986) found BZs to be effective in moderating acute stress responses in rats by affecting the amount of chloride ions in the benzodiazepine-GABA receptor complex in the cerebral cortical membranes.

Davidson (1993) found BZs effective against social-anxiety disorders compared with placebo treatments. A 2-year follow up also found them to be effective in the long term.

Lau et al. (1992) found BBs effective against cardiac disorders as they reduced high blood pressure in patients, leading to a 20% drop in risk of death.

Lindholm et al. (2005) found that although BBs reduced the risk of strokes, other hyper tension drugs were more effective.

21 SIT is a type of cognitive-behavioural therapy that cognitively restructures emotional and behavioural responses.

22 (i) *Assessment* — patient and therapist (i) reduce stressors into individual components (ii) consider how stressors are thought about and dealt with (iii) consider how successful these are, a common response being negative self statements that create a self-defeating internal dialogue.

(ii) *Stress reduction techniques* — patients are taught skills to deal with stress: self-instruction (instruction where coping self-statements are practised), direct action (where escape routes are arranged and relaxation exercises learned to reduce arousal), and cognitive coping (where positive coping statements are learned to counteract negative self-statements).

(iii) *Application and follow through* — patients practise using stress-reduction techniques as role play, then as real-life exercises, with stressors becoming increasingly more threatening.

23 Jay and Elliot (1990) found SIT effective in treating acute stressors, as teaching parents of leukaemia sufferers SIT skills resulted in less anxiety and better coping skills than teaching child-focused interventions.

Holroyd et al. (1977) found SIT effective in treating chronic stressors, as SIT patients had better relief of tension headaches than those receiving physiological treatments.

Holcomb (1986) found SIT to be effective in the long term, as not only did it reduce symptoms of depression, anxiety and distress more than drugs, but 3 years later SIT patients had fewer hospital admissions for psychiatric problems.

Chapter 5

1 Compliance occurs where there is public, but not private, agreement with majority influence in order to gain approval/avoid rejection.

2 (i) Internalisation (ii) Compliance.

3 (i) Internalisation (ii) Identification.

4 Identification involves private and public acceptance of a group's attitudes and behaviours, while compliance only involves public acceptance, not private. Internalisation is stronger, as it is maintained without the presence or influence of the majority influence.

5 NSI sees conformity occurring to gain acceptance/avoid rejection and therefore does not necessarily involve true agreement, which ISI does, as it involves looking to others for guidance as to what is proper/correct behaviour.

6 Cognitive dissonance is an unpleasant feeling of anxiety created by simultaneously holding two contradictory ideas. Conformity reduces cognitive dissonance by altering conflicting cognitions, so they become compatible with each other.

7 Asch (1955) found an overall conformity rate of 32% in getting individual participants to conform to the obviously wrong answers of a majority group, with 75% of participants conforming at least once. NSI was involved as public, but not private, agreement occurred in order to gain acceptance/avoid rejection.

Jenness (1932) found individuals were influenced by a group estimate when assessing the number of beans in a jar. This involved ISI, as there was no obvious correct answer and participants looked to others for guidance.

Exam practice answers and quick quizzes at **www.therevisionbutton.co.uk/myrevisionnotes**

Bogdonoff et al. (1961) found that stress levels declined when participants conformed, which supports the idea that conformity occurred due to a reduction in cognitive dissonance by reducing the inconsistency between the two incompatible cognitions of one's own beliefs and the beliefs of others.

8 (i) Obedience can be a force for good, as society cannot function meaningfully without rules and laws that people follow, or recognition of which people hold legitimate authority and have the right to give orders. (ii) Obedience can be a negative force for destruction if people obey orders unquestioningly with harmful consequences.

9 *Aims:* To see whether people could be manipulated to obey destructive orders they didn't necessarily agree with.

Procedure: 40 volunteer American males aged between 20–50 years were ordered by a confederate researcher at Yale University to give increasingly severe shocks to an initially compliant confederate participant who refused to continue after 300 volts.

Findings: 100% of participants went to at least 300 volts, 62.5% went to 450 volts. Participants were distressed, argumentative and three had seizures, though some seemed unaffected.

Conclusions: People will obey destructive orders that go against their moral code. The 'Germans are different' hypothesis is wrong.

10 ● Victim is silent throughout — 100%

● Study replicated in run-down office — 48%

● Learner in same room — 40%

● Force learner's hand onto a shock plate — 30%

● Experimenter gives orders by phone — 20.5%

● Two dissenting confederate teachers are present — 10%

● Teacher only reads out questions, confederate gives shocks — 92.5%

11 *Situational factors:* People do not obey because of personality but because of aspects of the situation. In Milgram's study obedience was high at prestigious Yale University but low in a less prestigious run-down office block.

Perception of legitimate authority: People obey authority figures possessing symbols of power and status like the laboratory coat of Milgram's confederate 'experimenter'.

The agentic state: People see themselves as agents of an authority figure's wishes and give up personal responsibility of the autonomous state, transferring responsibility to the authority figure, such as the confederate 'experimenter' in Milgram's study.

Personal responsibility: If people are personally responsible for their actions (part of the autonomous state), obedience will decline. In Milgram's study obedience declined when the learner was in the same room, even more so when his hand was forced onto a shock plate.

Gradual commitment: The more people comply with small acts of obedience, the harder it becomes to refuse further orders with more severe consequences. After giving seemingly mild shocks of 15, 30, 45-volt etc shocks, it becomes increasingly harder to refuse to give more severe shocks.

Dehumanisation: It is easier to obey orders to harm those seen as lesser people. Some in Milgram's study commented 'he was so stupid he deserved to be shocked'.

12 Independent behaviour refers to resistance to conformity (non-conformity) and to obeying authority figures (disobedience).

13 Dissent is a form of resistance involving the presence of an individual or individuals who publicly disagree and go against the majority. Research:

Asch (1955) found that dissent frees people up to give true answers as the presence of a dissenting confederate caused overall conformity rates to drop from 32% to 5.5%.

Allen and Levine (1971) found dissent gives strong support to people to resist conformity, as conformity reduced even when dissenters weren't competent.

Baron and Byrne (1991) found it is easier to resist majority influence where dissent occurs earlier rather than later.

14 ● *Reactance* — when people's freedom of choice is restricted, they often respond with reactance (rebellious anger).

● *Ironic deviance* — if people believe the source of informational influence is not genuine, then they'll resist such influence.

● *Status* — individuals of higher status within a group are more likely to resist majority influence as low-status members, such as newcomers, are motivated to achieve higher status by conformist behaviour.

15 (i) *Decreasing agentic state:* Lowering an authority figure's perceived legitimate authority decreases the agentic state and increases the autonomous state, making obedience less likely. When the experimenter was not present in Milgram's study but gave orders by phone, obedience rates declined.

(ii) *Increasing personal responsibility:* Anything making individuals feel more accountable for their actions decreases the agentic state and thus increases the autonomous state, making obedience less likely. For example, when participants in Milgram's study could see the effects of their shocks, obedience rates declined.

(iii) *Systematic processing:* People are less likely to obey if they consider what they have been ordered to do. Marin et al. (2007) found that if participants were encouraged to consider unreasonable orders, they were less likely to comply.

(iv) *Morality:* individuals whose behaviour is based on ethical principles are more resistant to destructive obedience. Kohlberg (1969) gave moral dilemmas to participants in the Milgram study, finding those who based decisions on personal moral codes were less obedient.

(v) *Experience:* Individuals with experience of destructive obedience are less likely to obey. An electrician in Milgram's study refused to comply, as he was aware of what harm such voltages could do.

(vi) *Personality:* Certain characteristics are associated with resisting obedience. Milgram (1974) proposed the 'authoritarian personality', characterised as prejudiced against minorities, rigid, inflexible and submissive to higher-status individuals. Those with opposite traits are therefore more resistant to obedience.

16 Social change is the processes by which society changes beliefs, attitude and behaviour to create new social norms.

17 A group can change a negative image held by outsiders to a positive one by contributing positively to society and promoting their worth to the community.

18 (i) Rebellious role models show how obedience and conformity levels can be lowered through observation and imitation, decreasing the level of negative social change occurring.

(ii) Zimbardo proposed that individuals could be encouraged to indulge in positive actions by reversing gradual commitment, like gradually encouraging people in a step-by-step process to involve themselves in recycling household rubbish.

(iii) Nemeth and Chiles (1988) proposed that by exposing individuals to models of independent behaviour they are taught to become more independent and thus more resistant to attempts to promote conformity and obedience levels, which could incur negative social change.

19 Moscovici et al. (1969) found consistent minorities influence majority opinion, as participants exposed to the obviously wrong answers of a consistent minority were more likely to agree than those exposed to inconsistent minority answers.

Martin et al. (2003) found that cognitive processing of minority opinions leads to the formation of attitudes resistant to counter-persuasion, as messages with minority group support were more resistant to change than if supported by a majority group.

Martin and Hewstone (1996) found minority influence is a force for innovation and social change as minority influence led to more creative and novel judgements than majority influence.

Chapter 6

1 (i) Deviation from social norms:

- Not conforming to a society's expected forms of behaviour is abnormal.
- The definition creates a distinction between desirable and deviant behaviours.
- The definition permits clinical interventions to achieve 'normality', especially for those unaware of their deviancy.
- The definition gives a social dimension to abnormality, excluding from society those behaving in socially unacceptable ways.

(ii) Failure to function adequately:

- Abnormality involves a failure to cope with everyday life.
- Behaviour is abnormal when it causes distress that leads to dysfunction, like affecting the ability to work.
- The definition focuses on individual suffering, concentrating on personal experiences of mental disorders.
- The definition permits individuals to decide themselves if they are abnormal, though others can also judge if a person is not coping.
- Personal dysfunction has seven features: personal distress, maladaptive behaviour, unpredictability, irrationality, observer discomfort, violation of moral standards and unconventionality. The more features an individual has, the more they are abnormal.

(iii) Deviation from ideal mental health:

- Abnormality is an absence of well-being.
- Jahoda (1958) proposed six categories of behaviour people should display to be normal: positive self-attitude, self-actualisation, autonomy, resisting stress, accurate perception of reality and environmental mastery. An absence of these criteria indicates abnormality.

2 (i)

- Individuals who do not conform to society's norms may not be abnormal but merely individualistic.
- Violation of social norms can be an excuse for influential groups to intervene in the lives of non-conformists seen as challenging such groups' influential positions in society.

(ii)

- A person's behaviour may cause others distress and be perceived as abnormal, while the individual themself feels little or no distress.
- An individual's apparently dysfunctional behaviour may actually be rewarding. For example, a person's eating disorder can bring attention and sympathy from others.

(iii)

- Most people would be considered abnormal, as it is difficult to realise all six criteria simultaneously.
- Jahoda's criteria are vague and thus difficult to measure.

3 Cultural relativism is the idea that definitions of what is 'normal functioning' vary cross-culturally and are equally valid.

4
- The deviation from social norms definition is culturally relative, as it relates to only one particular culture's view of social norms.
- Definitions of 'inadequate functioning' differ across cultures and we should not use what's inadequate in our own culture to judge others of different cultural backgrounds.
- The criteria used to judge deviation from ideal mental health are culturally bound (specific to one culture) and should not be used to assess people of other cultural and sub-cultural groupings.

5 The biological model sees abnormality as mental illnesses caused by malfunctioning biological processes, specifically in the structure and workings of the brain, the nervous system, genetic influences and the biological environment.

6 (i) *Infections/viruses*: Hideyo and Moore (1913) found the syphilis bacterium in brain tissue samples taken from patients who died from the degenerative mental disorder, paresis.

(ii) *Biochemistry*: Janowsky (2009) found a connection between abnormal neurotransmitter levels and developing depression and manic-depression. High levels of acetylcholine were associated with depression and low levels with mania.

(iii) *Genetics:* Weinberger et al. (2002) found the COMT gene was linked to an elevated risk of schizophrenia, by depleting the frontal lobes of the brain of the neurotransmitter dopamine, leading to hallucinations and an inability to perceive reality.

(iv) *Brain damage:* Tien et al. (1990) found that heavy and prolonged abuse of cocaine and/or amphetamines leads to brain damage and psychosis. Symptoms include hallucinations, delusions, thought disorders and personality changes.

7 (i) *Psychodynamic model:* The psychodynamic model is a psychological approach that perceives mental disorders as arising from unresolved, unconscious childhood disorders. These are repressed into the unconscious mind but affect conscious behaviour.

(ii) *Behavioural model:* The behavioural model sees maladaptive behaviour occurring through the learning processes of classical conditioning, where a response is associated with a certain stimulus; with operant conditioning, where abnormal behaviours are reinforced and so re-occur; and with social learning, where abnormal behaviours are observed and imitated through vicarious reinforcement.

(iii) *Cognitive model:* The cognitive model is a psychological approach perceiving mental disorders as due to negative thoughts and illogical beliefs, with such maladaptive thought processes leading to maladaptive behaviours. For example the cognitive triad consists of three illogical thought processes that can lead to irrational, negative emotions, resulting in depression.

8 Psychiatric drugs reach the brain by entering the bloodstream to modify behavioural effects, by increasing or decreasing the availability of neurotransmitters. Antagonists block the effects of neurotransmitters, while agonists mimic or increase neurotransmitter effects.

9 Furukawa et al. (2003) found antidepressants to be appropriate for treating depression, as a review of 35 studies showed antidepressants were more effective than placebos.

Bergqvist et al. (1999) found the anti-psychotic drug Risperidone had a dopamine-lowering effect that made it effective in treating obsessive-compulsive disorder.

10 ECT is mainly used to treat depression, but is also a treatment for schizophrenia.

11 A general anaesthetic and a muscle-relaxant are given before treatment, so that patients do not feel pain or convulse and incur fractures. Brain stimulation occurs through electrodes on the head, with a brief, controlled series of electrical pulses of between 70–150 volts, causing a brain seizure lasting about one minute. After 5–10 minutes, the patient regains consciousness. Brain stimulation can either be unilateral (to the non-dominant hemisphere) or bilateral (to both hemispheres).

12 Pagnin et al. (2008) found ECT to be a valid therapy for depression, as a meta-analysis of studies comparing the effectiveness of ECT, antidepressants and placebos in treating the condition found ECT superior in treating severe and resistant forms.

Tang et al. (2000) found that ECT does have beneficial uses sometimes as a treatment of schizophrenia, as ECT was effective in treating schizophrenics who didn't respond positively to anti-psychotics.

13 (i) *Psychoanalysis:* Psychoanalysis uses various techniques to allow patients insight into the origins of their disorders, which are seen as occurring through repression of events in the past. Dream analysis reveals inner conflicts through the symbolic latent content of dreams, while with free association patients speak freely to reveal a 'stream of consciousness' that psychoanalysts analyse to reveal repressed memories.

(ii) *Systematic desensitisation:* SD is a behavioural therapy that modifies phobias by constructing and working through a hierarchy of anxiety-producing stimuli. SD believes it is impossible to experience the two opposite emotions of fear and relaxation together, so uses classical conditioning to gradually replace irrational fears with incompatible responses of relaxation. Patients are taught deep muscle relaxation strategies and use these in rising stages of intensity, from weakest to strongest, when faced with the phobic object/situation.

(iii) *CBT:* CBT involves challenging and restructuring abnormal ways of thinking into useful, rational ones. With REBT, patients are encouraged to practise positive modes of thinking by reframing, which involves reinterpreting negative thoughts in more positive, logical ways.

14 (i) *Psychoanalysis:* Andreoli et al. (1999) found that the usefulness of psychoanalysis is dependent on the quality of clinicians, as psychodynamic psychotherapy (where patients relive childhood experiences) was effective if delivered by skilled therapists. Leichsenring et al. (2004) found brief dynamic therapy (a simplified form of psychoanalysis) as effective as CBT in treating depression and, as CBT is the main treatment of depression, this gives considerable support to the therapy.

(ii) *Systematic desensitisation:* Klosko et al. (1990) found SD highly effective, as comparison of various therapies for the treatment of panic attacks found 87% of patients panic free after SD, 50% with the drug Alprazolam, 36% with a placebo and 33% with no treatment. Jones (1924) used SD to eradicate 'Little Peter's' phobia of white fluffy objects by presenting a white rabbit at ever closer distances each time the boy's anxiety levels lessened. Eventually he was content in the presence of the rabbit, a feeling which generalised to similar white, fluffy objects.

(iii) *CBT:* Kvale et al. (2004) found CBT to be effective, as a meta-analysis of treatment studies for patients with dental phobias found that 77% of patients regularly visited a dentist 4 years after treatment. Tarrier (2005) reported CBT to be an effective treatment of schizophrenia, finding evidence of reduced symptoms and lower relapse rates.